Supporting Language and Literacy 0–5

This book offers practical guidance for those supporting young children's language and literacy development. It describes the important features of early language development, providing a clear and accessible theoretical framework illustrated by practical examples taken from a wide range of early years settings.

Linking directly to the Early Years Foundation Stage, the book focuses on the principles of good practice that play a vital part in delivering the EYFS successfully. These are set within the context of how children learn to communicate and think through reading, writing, speaking and listening. Additional guidance is provided on supporting children for whom English is an additional language.

Features include:

- a range of reflective and interactive activities supported by photocopiable materials;
- extension tasks for group training;
- practical examples to link theory to practice;
- a specific reading list for each chapter.

Supporting Language and Literacy 0–5 is an ideal handbook for trainers and trainees in local authorities, colleges and universities. It is also a valuable resource for early years practitioners encouraging them to reflect on their own experiences and understand the direct impact they can have on children's learning.

Suzi Clipson-Boyles is an education consultant, trainer and author. She supports and offers guidance to schools and local authorities in the areas of school improvement, early years and drama.

Supporting Language and Literacy 0–5

A practical guide for the Early Years Foundation Stage

Third edition

Suzi Clipson-Boyles

Routledge
Taylor & Francis Group

LONDON AND NEW YORK

First edition published 1996 by David Fulton Publishers as *Supporting Language and Literacy: A Handbook for Those who Assist in Early Years Settings*

Second edition published 2001 by David Fulton Publishers as *Supporting Language and Literacy 3–8: A Practical Guide for Assistants in Classrooms and Nurseries*

This edition published 2010
by Routledge
2 Park Square, Milton Park, Abingdon, Oxon, OX14 4RN

Simultaneously published in the USA and Canada
by Routledge
270 Madison Avenue, New York, NY 10016

Routledge is an imprint of the Taylor & Francis Group, an informa business

© 2010 Suzi Clipson-Boyles

Typeset in Celeste by FiSH Books, Enfield
Printed and bound in Great Britain by MPG Books Group

British Library Cataloguing in Publication Data
A catalogue record for this book is available from the British Library.

Library of Congress Cataloging-in-Publication Data
Clipson-Boyles, Suzi.
Supporting language and literacy 0–5 : a practical guide for the early years foundation
stage / Suzi Clipson-Boyles. – 3rd ed.
    p. cm.
    Includes index.
    1. Language arts (Early childhood)–Great Britain–Handbooks, manuals, etc. I. Title.
    LB1139.5.L35C55 2010
    372.6–dc22
                                                                                    2009047622

ISBN10: 0-415-55853-0 (pbk)
ISBN10: 0-203-85118-8 (ebk)

ISBN13: 978-0-415-55853-2 (pbk)
ISBN13: 978-0-203-85118-0 (ebk)

Contents

Getting the most out of this book

Children's learning and development are influenced directly by the quality of interaction and support that adults provide. This book offers a starting point for improving your knowledge, skills and understanding in a vital aspect of children's development – their communication and thinking skills through spoken and written language. It is intended for use by those who work or are training to work in maintained, private, voluntary and independent settings providing education and childcare for children aged 0–5. The focus is on adult support for language and literacy learning within the framework of the Early Years Foundation Stage (EYFS).

Those who work with children need to understand not only *what* children are learning about language and literacy but also *why*, *how* and *when* they are learning. Chapter 1 begins by setting language and literacy into the context of the EYFS. It goes on to consider the wider implications including the significance of play, the development of thinking skills and the influence of supporting adults in early years settings. Chapter 2 is all about partnerships, in particular the working partnerships within early years teams, partnerships with parents and carers, and working with partner organizations and services. Chapter 3 looks at observation and assessment and the important part these play in planning quality learning experiences that will lead to good learning and development outcomes for children. Chapter 4 provides practical approaches to supporting children with English as an additional language. Reading this first will enhance and extend the guidance offered in subsequent chapters. The separate strands of speaking and listening, reading and writing are presented in the discrete chapters that follow, although the inseparable links between them are not forgotten. The broader contexts within which language and literacy are acquired by young children across different social and curricular contexts are considered throughout.

Is this the right book for you?

This book is intended to be a practical and reflective resource designed to meet the needs of three different groups:

1 **independent learners** – providing reading material and activities for those training to work or already working with babies and young children;

2 **trainers or facilitators** – providing activity ideas and reading for groups of learners who are training to work with babies and young children;

3 **interested non-professionals** – providing reading material for those who have an obvious interest in babies and young children, for example school governors and parents.

Read, reflect and do!

The book places a particular emphasis on active learning and reflection. Wherever possible, theoretical frameworks are illustrated by practical examples and situations to be found in early years settings. All chapters include activities that relate to what is being discussed. These are included to help link the theory to the reader's own experience, to revise what has been read and to use different learning styles to understand and process the content. Some of these activities are supported by photocopiable activity sheets at the back of the book.

The importance of discussion

For those who are using this book independently, it would be helpful to talk to others about the content and activities. This will help you to organize and digest your thoughts and understanding. Likewise it would be valuable to discuss and evaluate your own work and receive feedback on your ideas and professional practice. Responding positively to constructive feedback is an important part of continuous improvement, particularly when useful action points can be followed through successfully.

For those using the book as part of a group, the discussion can clarify your thinking and deepen your understanding. Applying the content to individual experience and sharing this with others adds value to the learning and, more often than not, can trigger additional ideas. At the end of each chapter there are suggestions on how trainers might develop some of the themes in group situations, providing discussion topics and additional activities more suited to collaborative learning. Suggestions for assignments are also included in these notes for group leaders.

Additional reading

Children's communication, language and literacy are extensive and complex areas and the information provided in this book can only represent the tip of a very large iceberg! The aim is to stimulate thinking and awareness and provide starting points for the development of good practice. In order to help learners take responsibility for extending their own learning beyond the limits of this book, an additional reading list is included at the end of each chapter. Any references to other work made during the chapter can also be found in those end-of-chapter lists. A list of useful websites, applicable throughout the book, is included at the end of Chapter 1.

Applying your learning to real situations

Linking what you read to real situations and children for some of the activities will further enhance your learning. The practicalities of this will, of course, depend on whether or not you are currently working in an early years setting. If you do not have direct access to children, it is strongly recommended that you arrange visits, either through your learning organization or independently. Schools and settings are usually appreciative of voluntary help, so approaching somewhere local is likely to meet with a warm response, providing you are clear about the purpose of your visits and have all the correct Criminal Records Bureau (CRB) checks in place and up to date.

The language of every child matters

This chapter begins with a brief overview of the statutory requirements relating to communication, language and literacy for children from birth to five years. These relate primarily to the Early Years Foundation Stage (EYFS) but reference is also made to the National Curriculum for five-year-olds in Year 1. It goes on to consider the wider implications of language and literacy in the early years including the significance of play and the development of thinking skills. It looks at how adults can support these processes effectively, and the environmental factors that help to facilitate communication and develop language and literacy skills.

Communication, language and literacy are central to our learning and development. In schools, not only is English a subject in its own right but it also underpins all other subject areas including personal, social and emotional development. Early years settings should provide enriching activities throughout the day that constantly challenge and improve children's knowledge, skills and understanding. Such opportunities are also ensuring continuity of the developmental processes that have already taken place at home. For children whose learning and development have been held back at home, for whatever reason, enhanced or accelerated provision is often needed to help them catch up, so that they get the best possible start to their education. It is equally important that from the age of five the National Curriculum is delivered through stimulating integrated experiences that are meaningful and enjoyable to children and which motivate them to engage with learning.

The radical changes to education and care provision for young children in recent years include extensive statutory requirements for communication, language and literacy. These are prescribed by the EYFS, which is for children from birth to five in all private, voluntary, independent and state settings, including the Reception year in maintained schools. Five-year-olds in Year 1 are required to follow the National Curriculum requirements for English. These are set into context in this chapter, but it is important that you are familiar with the full documents detailing the requirements. These should be read in conjunction with this book. Publications are listed at the end of the chapter if you wish to download from the internet or order your own copies, which are available free from the DCSF publications order line. They should also be available in the setting where you work and your local library.

Every Child Matters

In 2007, the government introduced the Children's Plan, 'a ten-year strategy to make England the best place in the world for children and young people to grow up' (DCSF, 2007). The plan puts families at the centre of their strategy, but also focuses very much on multi-agency working to promote the best possible outcomes for all children.

Every Child Matters is the framework arising from that plan (see Cheminais, 2008 for more detail). It sets out the government's aim for every child, whatever their background or circumstances, to have the support they need to:

- be healthy;
- stay safe;
- enjoy and achieve;
- make a positive contribution;
- achieve economic well-being.

Clearly, early years settings play a crucial role in providing high-quality support and learning opportunities to promote these outcomes. The EYFS framework was introduced in 2008 to ensure consistency and optimum levels of provision across all such settings.

The Early Years Foundation Stage (EYFS)

The EYFS is a statutory framework for all registered settings that provide education and care for children from birth to five. The purpose of the EYFS is to ensure high-quality provision that will help young children achieve the five *Every Child Matters* outcomes.

There are five key principles that underpin the EYFS approach:

1. setting standards;
2. promoting equality of opportunity;
3. creating a framework for partnership working;
4. improving quality and consistency;
5. laying a secure foundation for future learning and development.

The framework has two sets of requirements: the learning and development requirements and the welfare requirements. There are six areas of learning:

1. personal, social and emotional development;
2. communication, language and literacy;
3. problem-solving, reasoning and numeracy;
4. knowledge and understanding of the world;
5. physical development;
6. creative development.

Whilst these areas of learning are distinctly defined, there is a clear expectation that activities should be planned in ways that enable children to connect and integrate across the different subjects. Babies and young children do not compartmentalize the vast array of things they are learning continuously. For them, everything is connected. Great emphasis is placed upon following each individual child's interests and needs to build on the natural curiosity and exploratory drives that are so much a part of their development. Individual needs are central to the framework in order to ensure that all children are included and have equal opportunity to achieve well. The diversity of children and their families is celebrated and respected. Importance is also placed on assessment and observation, play, exploration and active learning. Partnership and relationships are a recurring theme throughout the framework as is the influence of the environment within which children learn.

The National Curriculum

There has been a statutory National Curriculum in England for 5–16 year olds since 1988 and language and literacy have always been central to the requirements. In 2009, following a full review and consultation (Rose, 2009), it was proposed that the primary curriculum subjects should be integrated into six areas of learning:

1   understanding English, communication and languages;
2   mathematical understanding;
3   scientific and technological understanding;
4   historical, geographical and social understanding;
5   understanding physical development, health and wellbeing;
6   understanding the arts.

This revised approach (statutory from 2011), aligns the curriculum much more closely with the areas of learning and development in the EYFS and provides a smoother transition from Reception to Year 1 than previously. The Programme of Learning for English is structured around three sets of curriculum progression: speaking and listening; reading; and writing. (From the age of seven, there is an additional requirement to learn a modern foreign language.)

In addition to the six areas of learning, each of which has its own programme, the Primary National Curriculum defines six 'Essentials for Learning and Life'. These are skills that are taught across the curriculum to promote confident and successful lifelong learning. Two of the six relate particularly to this book. They are:

1   **Literacy**: communicating effectively and responding critically to a wide range of information and ideas;
2   **Learning and thinking skills**: investigating, creating, communicating and evaluating.

The inclusion of these strands across all six areas of learning demonstrates how vital it is to integrate language and literacy into everything that children think, do and learn.

Why is language so central to our lives?

Language is such an integral part of our lives that we often take it for granted. Every day we engage in hundreds of thousands of complex interactions involving speaking, listening, reading, writing and signing. But what would life be like without language? No talk, no hearing the talk of others, no print, no books, no media, no vehicle for expressing our feelings and no framework for our thinking. And imagine life without mobile phones! The reality would be that we would feel more isolated from each other and our current ways of working, relating and thinking would not only be altered but also significantly reduced.

ACTIVITY 1.1 Thinking about the language you have used today   (Time: 10 minutes)

Close your eyes and think back to when you woke up this morning. Now try to replay all your actions since then as if it were a film. What have you said? What have you heard? What have you read? What have you written? Make four columns on a sheet of paper headed with those four questions and jot down all your actions and experiences no matter how small: for example: radio news; cereal packet; train timetable; asking for something in a shop; texting a friend. Notice how many different types of interactions there have been, and consider how they fall into different categories.

Figure 1.1 Talk is a vital part of human communication

Our spoken and written language are our major means of communication and is central to all we do (Figure 1.1). During the first four years of life, children learn language at an amazing rate, at a time when they are also learning about the world in which they live. If we are to develop and extend children's language in early years settings it is vital that we recognize and value what each child already knows so that we can build on this when planning for their continued progress.

There are numerous theories about how language is acquired but the most significant factor that researchers have commonly identified is that *language learning takes place when children are interacting with adults* (Wells, 1985). In everyday life such relationships are numerous. Early years settings and schools are not the only communities within which the child uses language among adults. Figure 1.2 illustrates examples of other contexts in which language is learned and used. Each of these presents the child with a range of different vocabulary, structures and meanings. The situations can also vary enormously in the purposes for which language is used, and most children learn to switch from one to another with remarkable skill.

ACTIVITY 1.2 Language communities (Time: 20 minutes)

Make a photocopy of Activity Sheet A. Choose three of the communities from the selection in Figure 1.2 and record some of the specific features of the language that might take place by thinking about vocabulary and purpose. An example has been completed for you on the activity sheet.

Language and learning

Language helps children's learning and learning helps children's language. By the age of 4, the complexity and fluency of language acquired represents a remarkable achievement, especially when we consider how challenging it can be for an adult to learn a new language. If we also consider how many other things a four-year-old knows and understands it becomes clear that a very complex set of processes must be taking place.

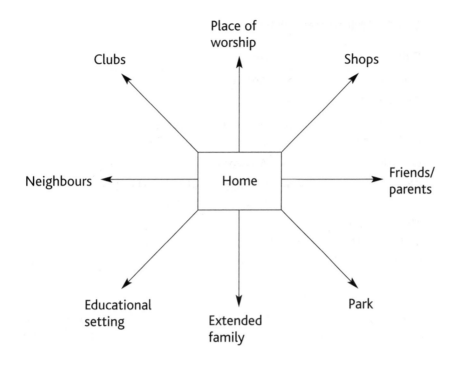

Figure 1.2 Other language communities for a young child

To help us identify some of those processes, it is useful to think about learning a second language to compare this with the language acquisition of young children. In a large-group situation, even the most dynamic of French teachers can only engage in direct exchange with one pupil at a time. The whole class chanting responses in unison is a technique used to increase the number of responses a pupil can make during a lesson, but what is missing from this type of exchange is spontaneity, individual adjustment and fluency of immediate response. A two-year-old at home with his or her primary carer, on the other hand, is engaging in a continuous stream of conversation. This will include a lot of repetition and reinforcement, and the language is likely to relate to the immediate interests and needs of the child. Let us look more closely at what might be assisting that two-year-old with his or her language development:

- intensive one-to-one interaction;
- engaging in a variety of tasks with associated language;
- language arising from curiosity and exploration;
- language relating to immediate stimuli;
- a range of environments and their associated language;
- a wide range of visual resources and artefacts;
- stories, rhymes and books.

We cannot assume that all home environments provide such rich and effective support for learning language. The quality of conversation, for example, can vary enormously, and this in turn affects the speed and sophistication with which a child's language might develop. In Table 1.1 we see a model of conversation where the adult responds to the child's question by developing a longer discussion. This enables the child to use a range of language and extend their thinking.

Table 1.1 Adult engages with the child and extends their talk

Child	Adult
Question 1 ⟶	Answer 1
Question 2 ⟶	Explanation
Repeats explanation ⟶	Approves and corrects this repetition
Question 3 ⟶	Answer 2
Challenges ⟶	Discusses and then asks child an open question
Thinks about and answers adult's question	

However, the second model, in Table 1.2, demonstrates how an adult might restrict the flow of a child's language by giving closed answers to questions, or even reprimanding the child for asking too many questions.

Table 1.2 Adult disengages with the child and prevents the talk from continuing

Child	Adult
Question 1 ⟶	Short answer 1
Question 2 ⟶	Reprimand

When we compare these two hypothetical examples we can see that the first adult has facilitated five additional units of conversation by the child following their original question. However, the second adult has closed down the potential for the child to use further language because they have reprimanded the child for asking a further question. This effect can also be caused by closed answers rather than receptive and opening listening and questioning by the adult.

It is a young child's job to ask questions; it is how they learn. Indeed the EYFS places great emphasis on planning experiences for children that arise from their individual interests and curiosity. If we multiply the number of child units by the number of times in any day when a child initiates talk, we can see that the child in the first example is going to have a vastly different experience from the child in the second example. If a child initiates language with an adult approximately 300 times in one day (this is a conservative estimate for a curious three-year-old), the child in Table 1.1 is likely to have 6 × 300 opportunities for talking, a total of 1,800 experiences, whereas the child in Table 1.2 is likely to have only 300. And these calculations are only for one day. Of course, this is a contrived mathematical exercise to illustrate the point and there will always be times when it is not appropriate or convenient to develop the conversation fully. Nevertheless, the example is intended to illustrate how significant the role of the adult is in providing opportunities and enabling experimentation and consolidation of young children's language. Where the language is exchanging backwards and forwards between adult and child, the child is hearing language spoken within a specific context. The child can therefore participate and experiment within that context using the language that is being modelled alongside the language he or she already knows.

As well as the amount of conversation, it is also necessary to consider the quality of the social relationship between child and adult. The child in Table 1.2 is experiencing not only fewer opportunities to hear and practise language, but he or she is also experiencing rejection and lack of respect as a learner. Which child do you think is most likely to feel frustrated and unvalued? It is easy to see how this type of relationship could lead to low self-esteem or negative behaviour.

Finally, it must not be forgotten that this example only accounts for the occasions when the child initiates the language. Adults also start conversations with children and it is obvious that this adds to the total number of language development opportunities a child might have in any one day.

ACTIVITY 1.3 Engaging children in discussion　　　　　　　　　　**(Time: 30 minutes)**

Imagine that a three-year-old child is sitting with their father on a bus. The child asks: 'Why does the bus keep stopping, Daddy?'. Using the frameworks in Tables 1.1 and 1.2, write an imaginary script for each, starting both with that same question. Think carefully about the sorts of things an adult and child might say in each example and consider the quality of what the father might say in terms of extending the child's own language. Consider what sort of reprimands or other comments from adults tend to close the conversation down. Think of three examples of closed questions by an adult in this situation and three examples of open questions.

Why is language important to children's thinking?

Do you ever talk to yourself when you are on your own? Most people do at some time or another. There can be different reasons for this according to the situation. Sometimes it might be a response to something that has happened or the actions or comments of another person ('Why do people rush through red lights like that? The world is going crazy!'). Sometimes it might be helping to organize our thinking ('Now what was I doing before the phone went? Oh yes! Close windows. Find car keys!').

Young children can often be observed talking to themselves. These narratives are the externalization of children's thought processes. For example, the child playing in the water tray might say, to no-one in particular, 'Ooooooh! Cold! That's cold, that is. Fill it up. Right to the top. Careful. Careful. Oh, oh – too much! Where's a bigger one?' We think in language, and therefore if our language is restricted then so is our thinking. When children are engaging in learning, whether these are planned or unexpected opportunities, the discussion is actually representing more than simple conversation. It is, in fact, assisting them with the organization and extension of their thinking. We think for many different reasons. For instance, we think in order to:

- plan ahead;
- remember back;
- solve problems;
- analyse, to help understanding;
- evaluate critically;
- choose a response;
- interpret meaning;
- create new ideas;
- create new meaning;
- reflect on experiences.

> **ACTIVITY 1.4 Promoting children's thinking** (Time: 10 minutes)
>
> Choose four of the reasons for thinking from the list above. Jot down ideas of experiences you might provide for children to facilitate and encourage each type of thought. For example: TO EVALUATE CRITICALLY – children might be given different types of toy cars to see which one can travel the fastest.

Children need independent time during which they can explore and use their thinking skills. They need the space to put into practice what they are learning. However, children also need to be challenged in their thinking and experience new language from which they can continue to extend their own vocabularies and linguistic structures. Babies learn to talk by watching and listening to others talk. It is important, therefore, to consider the role adults who work with children play in modelling, challenging and supporting. Language can be supported in ways that extend their thinking.

How can adults model, support and extend children's language?

When we consider the relationship between babies and young children, and the adults who care for them, we know that some forms of interaction are particularly beneficial to a child's language development. These include:

- showing an interest in what the child has to say;
- showing respect for what the child knows;
- encouraging the child's own ideas;
- encouraging the child to explain, describe and evaluate;
- demonstrating good models of language;
- correcting through example rather than criticism;
- encouraging the child to experiment with language;
- asking open questions (i.e. which don't just have one correct answer);
- avoiding talking down to or patronizing the child;
- encouraging the child to demonstrate as he or she talks;
- listening well to the child without interrupting;
- drawing attention to a range of texts as well as books (e.g. signs, labels, packaging);
- reading and telling stories;
- talking about stories and books;
- playing with rhymes.

In a one-to-one situation, the adult should be extending the child's language a little beyond his or her previous range. In other words, the child learns something new that builds upon what he or she already knows. This idea of extending children's range of language is well documented in the seminal work of Vygotsky (1978). He suggests that adults who support children's learning should extend that learning beyond the children's *current* levels of achievement towards their *potential* levels of achievement. Vygotsky calls the area of learning between these two levels the 'zone of proximal development'.

How can the educational environment influence children's language?

One of the four key principles of the EYFS is to provide enabling environments within which children can learn and develop. In relation to communication, language and literacy, the requirements highlight five particular environmental features:

1 a rich variety of language and literacy resources that take account of children's interests, backgrounds and cultures;

2 time to make use of and enjoy those resources;

3 alternative resources for those who need them to ensure inclusive access for all;

4 time for conversation and thinking;

5 special support for those learning English as an additional language.

When children are interacting mostly with other children of the same age, the language is not necessarily extended as much as when they are interacting with older children or adults – in some cases their peers may even be restricting their language use because they have not yet reached the same level. When an adult is present, however, the level of language can be raised in a positive way.

Children who attend nursery or school for full days are spending a large part of their time in that environment so it is important that it is stimulating and nurturing of children's language, literacy and learning. If children are going to talk they need something worthwhile to talk about. If they are going to learn to read they need interesting and appealing texts. If they are going to learn to write they need opportunities to experiment and practise for real reasons. All these things need to take place in an environment that is supportive and encouraging so that the children develop confidence in their own abilities and actively seek to learn. The underlying principles of providing such an environment include:

● good organization that involves the children;

● independence in finding, using and caring for resources;

● decision-making opportunities;

● time to plan;

● time to evaluate;

● time to reflect.

They need to be provided with experiences that:

● motivate;

● build on and extend current knowledge;

● challenge;

● involve active participation;

● involve different types of talk;

● have a meaningful purpose;

● require language and literacy in meaningful ways;

● are safe;

● allow exploration and scope to follow curiosity;

● allow the children to ask questions;

● allow the children to refer to texts;

● allow the children to experiment with and create texts.

Children need to value themselves as learners if they are going to be motivated and positive about learning. They need to be recognized for their achievements and encouraged to learn through their mistakes. This type of environment cannot be created by displays and resources alone; it is created through the attitudes and approaches of the adults in that environment for it is they who can make such a remarkable difference to the quality of children's experiences, learning, progress and welfare. Understanding *how* children learn best is an essential requirement of adults who support their learning. Play-based learning has long been a recognized feature of good early years practice and is central to the EYFS.

Language and play

Effective early years practitioners know that with careful planning and preparation play and learning can actually become one and the same thing. Children can learn an enormous amount through play and much of that learning relates directly to language. Play is a complex area to understand, and further reading on this subject is highly recommended (see Moyles, 2010). However, to encourage you to think beyond the surface features of play activities and into the deeper realms of the language learning that might be taking place, Table 1.3 illustrates some typical activities and the potential they offer for language and literacy. Clearly, there would be many more complex learning processes taking place and many sorts of language. Just one example for each experience has been highlighted here to exemplify.

Table 1.3 Language, literacy and play

Experience	Potential for language and literacy learning
Water play	Concept development through exploration
Puppet play	Exploring language of stories
Home corner	Exploring language of adults
Role play corner	Exploring new vocabulary
Paint play	Use of descriptive language
Clay play	Planning
Multilink	Use of mathematical language

Integrated and discrete experiences

Language and literacy are woven into the very fabric of all areas of learning in early years settings. Where language activities take place during another area of learning (e.g. planning to make models of dinosaurs may require looking at a non-fiction text for information), they are referred to as *integrated approaches to language.*

ACTIVITY 1.5 Play and language   **(Time: 40 minutes)**

Using copies of Activity Sheet B, carry out separate 10–minute observations of children's language during play. These can be the same child in three different play situations or three different children repeating the same play activity at separate times. Record the types of language and types of thinking that are taking place.

Where language activities are planned in their own right for specific language learning to take place (e.g. listening to stories) they are called *discrete language activities.*

This chapter has mainly discussed language and literacy as features of integrated learning. Indeed, an integrated approach is the most natural and meaningful way for young children to learn. But in order to understand fully the components of language and their implications for supporting adults, it is also important to understand speaking and listening (oracy) and reading and writing (literacy) as discrete subject areas, and these are addressed in Chapters 5–8. First of all, however, Chapter 3 looks at assessment, observation, recording and reporting – all vital components in ensuring that children's needs are accurately identified to inform the continuous cycle of planning for learning. Chapter 4 discusses approaches for children for whom English is an additional language. It is recommended that you read that chapter before reading the others so that you can apply what you have learned to everything you read subsequently.

Notes for group leaders

Extending the listed activities

- Activity 1.1 – Discuss in pairs to see how many different ways the events can be categorized or sorted. Is there a predominant language form?
- Activity 1.2 – Start the activity by sharing examples of how they change their language according to their audience. Do children do the same, or are they less aware of social sensitivities?
- Activity 1.3 – Role play some of the scripts in pairs for the rest of the group. Discuss how the child might feel in each situation. Share examples of questions from adults that open up, rather than shut down, the conversation.
- Activity 1.4 – Discuss the examples and cross-reference to Chapter 5 where different types of talk are provided.

Activities for assessment

- Design an interactive display activity on a given theme.
- Plan a play activity with literacy particularly in mind.
- Activity 1.5 – Analysis of these observations could provide the basis for a written assignment.

Additional topics for group discussions

- Discuss types of learning experiences that relate to each of the *ECM* outcomes.
- Share some ideas for creating a text-rich environment in nursery and in a childminder's home.
- What language games for babies have you seen used effectively?
- Research and discuss different languages and cultures that can be found in Britain.
- How might you provide writing activities through play?
- Share examples of activities that teach specific aspects of language.
- Discuss how language activities might be planned to take place within other areas of learning.

References and further reading

Bruce, T. (2005) *Early Childhood Education* (3rd Edition). London: Hodder Education.

Bruce, T. and Spratt, J. (2008) *Essentials of Literacy from 0–7 Years*. London: Sage.

Cheminais, R. (2008) *Every Child Matters: A Practical Guide for Teaching Assistants*. London: David Fulton Publishers.

DCSF (2007) *The Children's Plan: Building Brighter Futures*. Norwich: DCSF.

DCSF (2008) *The Early Years Foundation Stage* (Pack and CD-ROM). Nottingham: DCSF Publications.

Eyres, I. (2009) *English for Primary and Early Years: Developing Subject Knowledge*. London: Sage.

Moyles, J. (2010) *The Excellence of Play* (2nd Edition). Milton Keynes: Open University Press.

Murray, L. and Andrews, L. (2005) *The Social Baby: Understanding Babies' Communication from Birth*. Richmond, Surrey: CP Publishing.

Vygotsky, L. S. (1978) *Mind in Society: The Development of Higher Psychological Processes*. Cambridge, MA: Harvard University Press.

Wells, G. (1985) *Language, Learning and Education*. Windsor: NFER-Nelson.

Useful websites

Every Child Matters:
www.dcsf.gov.uk/everychildmatters/

Download the EYFS pack:
www.nationalstrategies.standards.dcsf.gov.uk/node/157774

DCSF publications order link:
http://publications.dcsf.gov.uk/

EYFS and related materials:
www.nationalstrategies.standards.dcsf.gov.uk/earlyyears

National Childminding Association:
www.ncma.ork.uk

Pre-school Learning Alliance:
www.pre-school.org.uk

Primary National Curriculum:
www.curriculum.qcda.gov.uk

Teachernet links to aspects of the EYFS including information for parents:
www.teachernet.gov.uk/teachingandlearning/EYFS

Under 5s – an independent UK site promoting early learning:
www.underfives.co.uk

Useful links for practitioners and parents including the influence of early language and literacy development on later years:
www.literacytrust.org.uk/database/earlyyears.html

The synergy of partnerships

This chapter is about working partnerships that can contribute to better outcomes for young children. It covers three main aspects. Firstly, it focuses on the nature and dynamics of working teams in early years settings. You are encouraged to analyse your own roles within past and present working relationships and to reflect upon your responses to others in teams and meetings. Secondly, it looks at partnerships with parents and carers – a vital contributing factor to promoting children's good learning and development. Finally, it discusses the value of partnerships with other organizations, services and providers.

Partnership in education

Partnerships can have a powerful impact on outcomes for babies and young children. Gone are the days when teachers worked alone with their classes behind closed doors. Their work is now often supported by other adults in the classroom, including an extensive professional workforce of teaching and learning assistants. This mirrors the longer-established model of nursery teacher and nursery nurse. It is also widely recognized that the involvement of parents and carers in their children's learning positively affects learning. Schools and early years settings work with other services and organizations for the benefit of children. Childminders have worked closely with parents and carers for many years, because of the nature of the relationship, but they have often been lone workers.

The working together of two or more people, organizations, or 'things', when the result is greater than the sum of their individual effects or capabilities, is known as 'synergy'. Imagine eating the ingredients of a Victoria sandwich, but eating them separately – butter, flour, sugar, raw eggs and jam. Then compare this with eating the cake itself – a miraculous transformation of substances into a different and delicious form. Partnerships are similar. Each partner, whether it is an individual or an organization, has something different to offer and the effect becomes much more than merely the sum of the individual parts. Indeed, it can have a power and energy of its own that enhances the quality of the work in a most effective way, and this is beneficial to children and adults alike.

> **ACTIVITY 2.1 Different types of partnership** (Time: 15 minutes)
>
> Use Activity Sheet C for this task. Think about a setting where you have worked or gained work experience. Think of the different partnerships that might be included in the categories listed on the sheets. Against each one, write down the possible impact this could have on outcomes for children.

How do you work and respond in working partnerships?

Those who assist in early years settings can have very different experiences of partnership working according to the ethos and policies of the workplace, and the leadership style of the teachers or managers. Some teachers give their assistants enormous responsibility and opportunities for decision-making, whereas others prefer to keep total control of everything. The latter approach is becoming less common because of the obvious benefits of collaborative planning, decision-making and delivery.

In early years settings and schools there is, inevitably, a managerial structure, but the relationships, nevertheless, require shared values and common goals that are reached by a clear commitment to working together. Partnership is most effective when all parties understand each other through clear communication, and where decision-making is made through consultation, discussion and honest feedback. Trust and mutual respect are also important elements of partnership, and where all these things are in place, a strong and effective bond can be formed. This is most likely to result in higher-quality support for children's learning, and ultimately better outcomes. Let us now consider the contribution that *you* make to *your* working partnerships.

When one works closely with another person in the way that teachers and assistants do, it is important to consider the nature of that partnership in order to identify how one's own contribution affects the success of the working relationship. For example, whilst the teacher ultimately has the responsibility for the quality of provision, other members of the team should feel they can make suggestions. They have much to offer that can enhance the quality of provision, and everyone brings a different perspective. Good teachers and managers value what each member of the team can bring to the partnership.

In other words, even if you do not feel you have as much decision-making power within your working partnership, you do have an equal responsibility to ensure that the relationship is positive and effective, and the ways in which you relate and respond to your fellow team members will have a significant impact on the day-to-day quality of your work.

> **ACTIVITY 2.2 Evaluating your working partnerships** (Time: 30 minutes)
>
> Using Activity Sheet D, consider each question in relation to your current working partnership, or one that you have experienced in the past. Do you feel able to share these thoughts with that partner? If not, ask yourself why and consider if there is anything you could do to change this.

Partnerships within teams

Teams in early years settings and schools have become larger and more complex in recent years. Teams are interesting; they are composed of personalities and roles that can lead to a complicated set of interpersonal relationships. In order to develop an awareness of how you work within your team, and why, we will now look more closely at some of the important facts about teams.

The synergy of teams

There are many types of teams, and those that exist in early years settings are frequently composed of a wide variety of adults: teacher; nursery nurse; paid assistant; unpaid voluntary assistant; parent; governor; student; playgroup leader; and special needs support assistant, to name the most obvious. Teams also vary in the way they operate – some show real cohesion and solidarity, but in rare instances others can sometimes hold the discomfort of resentment and dissatisfaction.

Early years teams operate at their best where all the members have a commitment to the fact that they are a team and really value working together. They hold a shared vision that springs directly from the needs of the children. Other notable features of effective early years teams are:

- commitment to securing the best outcomes for children;
- continuous evaluation to drive improvement;
- clarity of purpose and direction coupled with high expectations;
- clear understanding of roles and responsibilities;
- direct and effective communication;
- flexibility and adaptability;
- early identification of problems and agreed action for solutions;
- clear time plans and deadlines;
- well-organized systems;
- recognition of the team's strengths and weaknesses;
- regular self-assessment of how the team is functioning;
- meetings that are efficient and effective.

What makes a good team member?

We would not all expect to have the same skills in a team. Just as the cake needs the right balance of different ingredients, so the team benefits from the variety of skills and attitudes that each individual member brings to it. Nevertheless, it is useful to develop a clear understanding of the general principles that strengthen a team through the quality of the relationships. An ideal team member does not necessarily follow unquestioningly, merely performing duties and obeying orders. Such passive behaviour does nothing to help the growth and development of a team and its work. Instead, a team member will contribute constructively and creatively in four main ways.

1. Belief system

A good team member:

- believes in securing the best outcomes for the children in their care;
- is committed to the overall success of the team in achieving that aim;
- respects the leader but does not expect that leader to take all the responsibility;
- has high expectations of the team's work in providing high-quality opportunities for children's learning and development.

2. Self-awareness

A good team member:

- knows their own strengths and skills;
- knows their own limitations;
- recognizes areas for development in their own practice;

- is aware of their role within the group;
- knows when to ask for help and advice;
- can accept criticism positively as a means of doing better.

3. Social skills

A good team member:

- supports the needs of others;
- is a good listener;
- is aware of impact on others;
- does not avoid problems;
- is committed to exploring conflict and resolving difficulties;
- recognizes the importance of open and honest relationships;
- respects the feelings of others;
- respects different viewpoints;
- knows when it is appropriate to speak up;
- knows when it is more helpful to keep quiet.

4. Professional skills

A good team member:

- takes advice constructively;
- gives advice constructively;
- communicates clearly;
- works with and not against others;
- thinks creatively;
- can demonstrate flexibility;
- shares the responsibility of decision-making;
- is clear about their role but is not inflexible;
- can work independently without undermining the work of the team;
- reflects and builds continuously on own performance and practice.

ACTIVITY 2.3 What sort of team member are you?   (Time: 20 minutes and ongoing)

Think about the team in which you work. If you are not currently in post, think about your training group. Look at the list of characteristics of a good team member above. Assess how good you are. What do you do well? Where do you need to improve? Do not overwhelm yourself with too many things all at once. Perhaps take one area of focus each week.

Team meetings

Regular meetings are essential to the effective communication of any team. The seven main purposes of meetings, though not necessarily every time, are:

1 to plan for future work;
2 to share information including assessments;
3 to identify and solve problems;
4 to make decisions;

5 to maintain a sense of group belonging;

6 to evaluate the effectiveness of the provision;

7 to identify areas and plan for improvement.

The usefulness of such meetings will depend on the team leader to a certain extent, but it is also the responsibility of all team members to ensure that meetings are productive. Teams in which members merely follow their leader's instructions tend to be less productive than those that share and explore ideas with everyone.

ACTIVITY 2.4 Reflecting on your responses in meetings   (Time: 10 minutes)

Pause to think about how you respond in meetings. What role do you take? How do you contribute to discussions? How do you feel about the contributions of others? Is there anything you could do better?

Team conflict

All teams can expect to experience conflict sometimes. Conflict is inevitable and it is essential that it should be dealt with rather than avoided. However, the way in which teams deal with the conflict can make a significant difference to the outcome and the future health of the team.

It is important to recognize and acknowledge conflict when it arises, to discuss it and to try to understand what is really at its root. One way to start is to identify the areas of agreement and disagreement. This is useful to the team because it creates a better understanding, not only of issues but also of each other.

Exploring conflict can be a creative process. Where a satisfactory solution is the outcome, all the team will benefit from a sense of achievement. This will strengthen the team and create healthy growth as opposed to leaving the area of disagreement in a dark corner where it will lurk and fester.

Partnerships with parents and carers

Parents are their children's earliest and longest-standing educators. They have a vast knowledge that can contribute to the work of practitioners. Research has shown time and time again that when parents are involved in their child's learning they are likely to make better progress (National Literacy Trust, 2001). Where practitioners can share information and advice with the parent, this can be used to benefit the child at home, thus forming a continuous link to strengthen the child's experiences. Such partnership can have a hugely positive impact on children's learning and development. Effective communication leads to better understanding in both directions. For example, when a parent provides information about a child's interests, this can be used creatively to plan learning opportunities. Likewise, when a discussion takes place about behaviour, practitioners can share good practice strategies for the parent to apply at home so that the child's experience is consistent.

There are many factors to consider when planning for effective partnerships with parents and carers, in particular providing:

- a welcoming environment that facilitates easy discussion;
- a culture that assures parents and carers that their views are valued;
- useful information about what is provided and expected;
- good-quality information about the child's achievement and development;
- opportunities for parents and carers to discuss and contribute to children's profiles;
- support with helping children to learn and develop at home;

- additional support and opportunities for hard-to-reach parents and carers;
- respect for diversity and equal opportunities for all.

> **ACTIVITY 2.5 Respecting diversity** (Time: 10 minutes)
>
> Not only is every child different but so also is every family. Make a list of the ways in which families might differ, then think carefully about the things you would need to do to help them feel welcome and valued in your setting.

Partnerships with other organizations, services and providers

Links and collaboration with partner organizations and services can do much to improve outcomes for children. They may enrich the curriculum provision; for example a visit from the local Chinese chef to cook and share food could bring tremendous learning across different areas, including cultural awareness. The point needs to be made here that the impact of such experiences should be carefully evaluated to ensure that they are making a difference. Likewise, partnerships with health or social services can do much to improve the well-being and development of young children, particularly those in vulnerable groups. Improving behaviour, support with language or support on safeguarding issues are all examples of areas where additional support, guidance or intervention might be extremely beneficial. The EYFS framework has done much to encourage greater partnership at all levels, not least between different providers of childcare and education. Where a child transfers from one provider to another, or in some cases attends more than one setting, good communication and collaboration is crucial to the continuous progress of that child.

Notes for group leaders

Extending the listed activities

- Discussions about the activities in this chapter should be carried out in pairs, rather than opening them up to a larger group, because this is likely to provide a safer framework within which to share what may be quite personal thoughts and feelings. Wherever possible, try to precede this with a general discussion about giving peer support or, for example, how one can best help and encourage one's partner through such discussions.

- Group work is very appropriate for examining team skills. Team-building activities in groups of four could include:
  - building a structure from newspapers to support a wine bottle;
  - writing a short play script to perform for children;
  - planning a party for the group with a theme;
  - evaluating how well they work together as a group and, if necessary, making some improvements.

- Observing and discussing roles within the team after the activity is as useful as the team activity itself. Sometimes it can be useful to have an observer making notes during a group activity.

Activities for assessment

- Produce an agenda for a team meeting and explain what you would hope to achieve for each item. How would these contribute to the outcomes for children?

- Research multi-agency partnerships and write about the impact of those in order to evaluate how effective they are.
- Research and write about a particular culture and show how this information could improve the partnerships with families.

Additional topics for group discussions

- Where might partnerships with other agencies be important in relation to safeguarding?
- Discuss ideas on how you might make contact with hard-to-reach parents.
- Why is it important to build good partnerships with other childcare and educational settings?
- Research and discuss networks that can help reduce isolation for childminders.

References and further reading

Baldock, P., Fitzgerald, D. and Kay, J. (2009) *Understanding Early Years Policy*. London: Sage.

Cheminais, R. (2006) *Every Child Matters: A Practical Guide for Teachers*. London: David Fulton Publishers.

Cousins, L. (2006) *Be a Better Nursery Nurse*. London: Teach Books.

Fox, G. (2003) *A Handbook for Learning Support Assistants*. London: David Fulton Publishers.

Knowles, G. (2009) *Ensuring Every Child Matters*. Ilkley: Sage.

National Literacy Trust (2001) *Parental Involvement and Literacy Achievement: The Research Evidence and the Way Forward. A review of the Literature*. London: NLT.

TDA (2006) *Induction Materials for Teaching Assistants in Primary Schools*. London: TDA Publications.

Walton, A. and Goddard, G. (2009) *Supporting Every Child: A Course Book for Foundation Degrees in Teaching and Supporting Learning*. Exeter: Learning Matters Ltd.

Observation, assessment and planning

This chapter is about the crucial roles that observation and assessment play in improving outcomes for children. It explains how good linkage between assessment and planning should lead to a positive impact on children's learning and development. Having set the context of individual differences between children, the chapter goes on to explain the importance of good practice in assessment and planning. It then outlines the practicalities of observation and recording, including why assessment information needs to be shared between practitioners, settings, parents and carers and, of course, the children themselves. There is an overview of the Early Years Foundation Stage (EYFS) statutory assessment framework which should be read in conjunction with the more specific detail of the EYFS Profile Handbook (QCA, 2008a). The link to Key Stage 1 is also explained. There is a glossary of common terminology relating to assessment at the end of the chapter – it would be a good idea to look at this first!

Every child is different

If all children were predictable in their progress, moving through exactly the same stages at exactly the same times and responding in identical ways to the same experiences, there would be no need for assessment. We could simply refer to a table of figures, read off the correct level for the child's age and select a one-size-fits-all package of learning. How mechanical that would be – measuring a production line of clones! In reality, children are much more interesting than that. They are born with unique genetic profiles and have very different social, emotional and cognitive learning experiences from the day they are born that influence their progress. As a result, when they arrive at their childminder, preschool, nursery or school, even if they have similar dates of birth, they might be at quite different stages of development. They will also bring with them a varied set of cultural values, attitudes and approaches to learning. If the education in those settings is to be relevant, meaningful and sufficiently challenging for each individual child, it is important for all who work with them to recognize and understand their needs. That process requires careful observation and monitoring with clear communication of information between everyone concerned.

> **ACTIVITY 3.1 Every child is different** (Time: 10 minutes)
>
> Make a list of the ways in which children are different from each other that will need to be considered when planning for their learning and development.

Improving outcomes for children

The EYFS is designed to give all children an equal opportunity to develop a good foundation for their future learning. When they reach the end of Reception, children's levels of attainment across all areas of learning have to be reported to their local authority. This is a statutory requirement. Children's attainment is then compared, locally and nationally, to ensure that every child, and all groups of children, are reaching their full potential. Results for communication, language and literacy (CLL) and personal, social and emotional development (PSED) are used in particular by local authorities and government as significant indicators to identify individuals and groups that are most at risk. These early assessments help schools to put in place appropriate intervention strategies to help those children catch up. You will not be surprised to read that there are many gaps, showing that some children, and certain groups of children, are behind. Closing the attainment gap is everyone's responsibility in order to give all children the best start, and preparation for their future economic well-being. Assessment is therefore vital, not only to identify the learning needs of each individual and measure their progress but also to ensure that planning is accurate and appropriate.

Roles and responsibilities

Everyone who works with young children has a statutory responsibility to assess their progress in order to provide appropriate learning opportunities and experiences. Childminders, for example, should regularly adapt and develop their daily provision to meet the changing needs of children in their care. This works best when it is based on their daily observations. Adults who work as part of a team in early years settings will normally be expected to contribute to overall assessments through observations. This approach brings a range of perspectives and the observations contribute valuable information to the teacher's or manager's bank of summative information about each child. The legal responsibility to submit final assessment information at the end of EYFS is normally carried out by the Reception teacher, and the headteacher has to ensure accurate reporting to the local authority. There are also expectations that good moderation procedures are followed to ensure that assessments are accurate. It is the role of the local authority to provide suitable training for assessment and moderation.

Why do we need to assess babies and young children?

Assessment plays a vital role in providing high-quality educational experiences for babies and young children. Not only does it help us to understand what they can already do and what they need to learn next but it also helps us to measure the progress they are making. More specifically, we need to assess them in order to:

- plan appropriate experiences so that learning is at the right level;
- measure progress to ensure that they are achieving their full potential;
- give feedback to the child and help them reflect on their own learning;
- identify when levels of additional support are needed;
- inform external agencies when needed;

- measure the effectiveness of the practitioners and provision;
- demonstrate the performance of the setting or school;
- inform parents/carers and involve them in their child's learning;
- inform the next provider, teacher, setting or school about what the child can already do so that they can build accurately on their strengths.

Good assessment in practice

The approaches used by practitioners to assess babies and young children, and how they then use that information can impact significantly on the quality of provision. This, in turn, influences the outcomes for the children. However, assessment has to be useful – there is no point in gathering information that will then sit in a file on a shelf. Formative observations and summative judgements about children's development and learning should be part of an active and interactive process. Characteristics of good assessment practice include:

- the use of regular and systematic planned observations;
- the inclusion of spontaneous observations when appropriate;
- summative assessments that are made on the basis of consistent and independent behaviours;
- taking account of the all-round picture of the child, including contextual information;
- involving parents and carers in the process;
- involving the children in the process;
- using assessment information effectively to inform planning;
- using assessment information to identify where additional support or intervention may be needed;
- using assessment information to evaluate the effectiveness of provision and plan for continuous improvement.

ACTIVITY 3.2 Parents' contributions to assessment   **(Time: 30 minutes)**

Look at the 'Practice Guidance for the Early Years Foundation Stage' (QCA, 2008a). Find the section on language for communication for birth to 11 months. How would you approach a discussion with parents to find out what a child can do at home? How might the information help you in your planning and resourcing?

Assessment and planning

It is vital to plan stimulating opportunities and experiences that challenge each child appropriately and meet their individual learning styles, needs and interests. The accurate assessment of children's skills, knowledge and understanding means that teachers can plan more effectively. Planning the right kinds of daily play opportunities and learning experiences at appropriate levels makes all the difference to how well the children achieve. If something is too hard for a child to grasp, they will get bored, frustrated, or give up. If something is too easy, they may also get bored and give up – certainly they will learn very little that is new. Either way, their learning is slowed down or held back. To prevent this happening, each child's daily learning needs to be pitched at a level that builds on what they already know to help them move along a pathway of progression and development. This will keep them interested and motivated, leading to a sense of achievement and higher self-esteem. However, such effective planning can only be possible if there is an accurate picture of where each child is in their learning and development, and the progress they are making. This is the primary reason for assessment – a useful tool that should be contributing towards better outcomes for children. In early years settings, observations are the building blocks for assessment.

Observation

Observing babies and young children enables you to track their progress so that accurate planning can take place for their continual development and learning. Observation involves watching, listening and recording, and should be happening throughout the day as you work and play together. It is important to plan observations systematically, thinking about focus, timing and context. However, unexpected events can also provide useful information about a child, so spontaneous observations also have a part to play.

Looking at the end-product of a child's efforts often tells us much less than if we have seen the processes through which the child reached that final stage. For example, while a child is painting a picture they might be learning the names of colours, talking about the composition of their picture and the consistency of the paint, and using fine motor skills to manipulate the paintbrush effectively. All of these could be missed if the only assessment was of the end-product, the finished painting. Observations can be carried out from a distance when the child is unaware that you are watching. On other occasions you may record your observations during an interaction. The following questions can provide useful markers for your observations:

- What did the child already know and understand?
- Was the task planned or unplanned?
- If it was planned, did the child know what was expected of him/her?
- If in a group, what was the composition of the group and how did the child respond to his/her peers?
- How much adult intervention was required during the activity?
- What new learning took place?
- Did the child experience any challenges to their learning? Why do you think this, and what was their response?
- Did the child have access to appropriate resources?

The last bullet point should not be underestimated. It would be most unfair to assume that a child was not very competent at cutting out, for instance, when, in fact, the scissors he or she was using were blunt. In other words, observations should always consider the context.

A single observation does not constitute a summative assessment. To confirm that a child has securely acquired a particular level or skill it is essential to see this consistently applied on more than one occasion.

ACTIVITY 3.3 Observing a child　　　　　　　**(Time: 5 × 10-minute slots in one week)**

Make a copy of Activity Sheet E. After preliminary discussions with the person responsible for the setting choose one child to observe. Spend ten minutes in each of the different social situations listed on the sheet. These observations might be carried out at various times across a one-week period. Make notes and comments each time about the child's responses, language and behaviour. When you have finished collecting your notes, compare them to see if there were differences between the child's responses. What did you notice about the child's speaking and listening skills?

Records and recording

Records can be useful for a range of purposes, and the format usually varies according to the function of the information. However, the production of records can be time-consuming and therefore they should be designed in ways that provide useful and easily accessible information, rather than unnecessary mountains of paper to which no-one ever refers. In other words, there is no point in recording for the sake of it. It needs to serve a useful purpose. It can be helpful to ask:

- Why am I doing this?
- How will it be useful?
- What do I need to record?
- Is there anything I can leave out?
- How can I record so it is easy to understand and analyse?
- How might I share the information with the child?
- How does it connect to the recording done by others?
- Can the records be easily interpreted by others?
- What will happen to my recording when I have completed it?

There are longer-term profiles of the child that accumulate, providing evidence over time of the child's achievements. A team approach to this type of record-keeping means that a variety of perspectives and types of evidence can be included, including those from the child and parents. This offers a more representative all-round picture of the child.

ACTIVITY 3.4 Creative systems for recording   (Time: 30 minutes)

Many settings use sticky notelets to record snapshots of children's actions. Think creatively about how these might be colour-coded and collected in ways that would be useful and easy to inform the next stages of planning. Design a system where different adults might contribute observations both systematically and spontaneously.

The reporting and sharing of assessment information

Teachers have a statutory responsibility to report information about each child's progress to a range of different people (e.g. parents, headteacher, government). Supporting adults have a professional responsibility to report to the following:

- **The children.** As you are working with children it is important to give them feedback on how they are doing. This can give them encouragement and help them reflect on their learning in order to make good progress. Getting children to talk about their own learning and assess, in their own way, how well they have performed on a task is known as 'Assessment for Learning'. This can be a very powerful tool because it gives the child a better understanding of what they are doing and why. It also motivates them by recognizing their achievements, and gives them ownership of the next steps.

- **The manager or teacher.** You will have many opportunities to observe certain things that the manager/teacher will not see because she or he is working with other children at the time. You therefore need to agree with the teacher how and when you will report back after working with particular groups. When working in a team, the sharing of assessment information between team members makes an important contribution to the ongoing planning.

- **Parents and carers**. It is likely that you will have a role as Key Worker for some children if you work in a larger setting. It will be your responsibility to share useful information about the children in your group with their parents or carers. This two-way discussion can enhance provision by helping everyone to understand the child's learning and development needs at that point.

It is also important to remember when not to report. Your knowledge of individual children should not be discussed outside the setting or school unless it is in a professional capacity at a meeting. Parents can, quite rightly, object to their child's behaviour being discussed with other parents in the playground for example.

Assessment and the EYFS

The EYFS provides a useful framework for assessment. It is a legal requirement for all providers to follow this framework. Each of the six areas of learning is assessed along a nine-point scale. However, there are 13 assessment scales rather than six because some areas have more than one scale. Personal, social and emotional development (PSED) has three scales. Communication, language and literacy (CLL) has four scales. Problem-solving, reasoning and numeracy (PSRN) has three scales. The four nine-point scales for CLL are:

1 language for communication and thinking;
2 linking sounds and letters;
3 reading;
4 writing.

At the end of Reception, children's scores on the 13 scales are recorded on the EYFS profile, which is shared with parents. The scores for every child are submitted to the local authority and this data is collated each year by the Department for Children, Schools and Families (DCSF). This enables schools and local authorities to measure how well different groups are achieving and identify where more support is needed to improve outcomes. For managers, the data can be extremely useful in comparing performance between the areas of learning, which will indicate strengths and weaknesses in the provision. Levels and expectations on the nine-point scales have not been included here due to the changing nature of averages each year. Please refer to the most up-to-date guidance on expected levels on the DCSF website.

The early learning goals

The early learning goals are the stages that most children are expected to reach by the end of the EYFS. Each area of learning has its own early learning goals, with some obvious connections between them. Some children will have exceeded those goals, and others will still be working towards them when they are assessed at the end of Reception. When children start the statutory part of their schooling in Year 1 the assessments to see how they are achieving in relation to these goals provides a baseline for the next stage of learning. This baseline helps Key Stage 1 teachers to measure their progress from then onwards as they follow the National Curriculum. The QCA booklet *Continuing the Learning Journey* (2006) provides useful information and training guidance on the use of assessment information for transition between EYFS and Key Stage 1.

Progression in the National Curriculum

Key Stage 1 covers the first two years of primary education, Year 1 following immediately after Reception. The EYFS profile assessments provide Year 1 teachers with relevant information to help them plan appropriate learning at the right level for each child, in order to ensure a smooth transition between the key stages. There is no statistically proven correlation between EYFS profile scores and National Curriculum levels. However, a child who has attained high scores at the end of the EYFS can usually be expected to reach more challenging learning objectives at the next stage and will therefore be working at higher National Curriculum levels. The National Curriculum enables teachers to assess children against national standards. There are three attainment targets for *Understanding English, Communication and Languages*: speaking and listening, reading and writing. Eight levels for each target describe what a child can be expected to know, understand and do at certain points. There is also a ninth level for exceptional performance. At the end of Key Stage 1, teachers have to submit their assessments to the national database. Children are expected to be achieving at around the average Level 2 by this stage, with more able children achieving the higher Level 3.

Inclusion

It is every child's right to have an equal opportunity to achieve well, regardless of their background, gender or ethnicity. As well as assessing children as individuals, assessment information provides a way of checking that all groups of learners are making sufficient progress. For example, are girls doing as well as boys? Are there variations between different ethnic groups? What about children with special educational needs or disabilities? Are looked-after children making as much progress as others? In settings that are large enough to identify particular groups it is vital for leaders and managers to check that the provision is meeting the needs of all so that they can achieve well. Where there are gaps between groups, this should be checked to see why, so that the provision can be adapted and strengthened; likewise, the progress of children with special educational needs and/or disabilities. This might relate to matters such as the curriculum, expectations of staff, provision for learning styles, approaches to teaching behaviour, cultural needs or means of communication, to name but a few. Where attainment gaps are evident, the next steps to consider should include:

- analysing why attainment is lower for that group or child;
- planning what action is required (e.g. staffing, programmes, external agency help, resources);
- involving the parents or carers;
- setting reasonable targets within a specified time-frame;
- monitoring and assessing the impact;
- making arrangements for regular review of provision.

> **ACTIVITY 3.5 Case study**   **(Time: one week)**
>
> In agreement with the setting manager and child's parents, select a child with special educational needs or a disability. Write a case study to include: the nature of their special needs; how their progress in learning and development compare with other children; the way provision is adapted to meet their needs; what difference that makes to their progress. If appropriate, arrange a discussion with the child's parent or carer.

Assessment glossary

The business of assessment has key terminology reflecting different approaches that are used for varying purposes. Here are some of the common terms:

- **achievement** – the progress a child makes in their learning and development from whatever is their starting point
- **assessment for learning** – where there are planned opportunities for the child to talk about and/or reflect on what they have learned in order to understand what they need to do next to improve
- **attainment** – standards actually reached in line with common measures: for example national average levels expected at the end of Reception
- **diagnostic assessment** – a focused assessment to gain more information about a specific aspect, often carried out in order to plan special intervention
- **differentiation** – adapting the learning according to each child's needs so that they are making good progress at the appropriate level; sometimes planning is differentiated by group, where several children may be working at a similar level
- **summative assessment** – where the child's performance is measured and summarized at a certain point, usually resulting in a score
- **formative assessment** – where the assessment information is used as an ongoing part of the teaching and learning, for example through feedback
- **informal assessment** – the everyday judgements that teachers and assistants make in order to fine-tune or adapt what has been planned
- **observation** – watching children as they are learning in order to note what they know and can do; can be planned as a formal observation or be spontaneous and informal
- **profile** – a collection of evidence and record-keeping that builds up over time to show the child's learning journey and where they are at that moment
- **running record/miscue analysis** – a diagnostic reading test where you count and analyse the pattern of mistakes that a child is making while reading aloud in order to identify which strategies need more support
- **standardized tests** – where the score can be calculated to show how the child relates to the norm (the test will have been measured on large numbers of children to show 'typical' results)
- **standards** – a certain level reached, usually measured against a local or national norm, so, for example, they may be below average or in line with the majority.

Notes for group leaders

Extending the listed activities

- Activity 3.2 – Pairs could prepare, write a script and perform a discussion between practitioner and parent as an alternative way of presenting their ideas to the rest of the group.
- Activity 3.4 – Ideas could be discussed in the group as a whole. A policy and practice document could then be produced.
- Bring in examples of recording formats for record-keeping to compare and discuss.

Activities for assessment

- Activities 3.3 and 3.5 provide the basis for a more detailed case study.
- Design a system for recording children's progress towards the early learning goals.
- Carry out a comparative analysis of the EYFS profile data from two different local authorities.

Additional topics for group discussions

- Discuss how often, when and why supporting adults should record information while working with children.
- Copy pages relating to CLL from the Practice Guidance for the EYFS and cut into pieces. Get the group to match the age ranges to 'Development matters' and 'Look, listen and note'. Discuss.
- Show and discuss examples of Key Stage 1 planning and assessments.
- Look at the e-profile on line.
- Look at your local authority's EYFS data compared to the national picture (available from the DCSF website).
- Share ideas of observation and recording systems seen in different settings.
- How do childminders keep records of children's progress?

Further reading

Glazzard, J., Chadwick, D., Webster, A. and Percival, J. (2010) *Assessment for Learning in the Early Years Foundation Stage.* London: Sage.

Hutchin, V. (2008) *Supporting Every Child's Learning Across the Early Years Foundation Stage.* London: Hodder Education.

Palaioloqou, I. (2008) *Childhood Observation.* Exeter: Learning Matters Ltd.

QCA (2008a) *Early Years Foundation Stage Profile Handbook.* London: QCA.

QCA (2008b) *Continuing the Learning Journey.* London: QCA.

Riddall-Leech, S. (2008) *How to Observe Children.* Oxford: Heinemann.

Children who speak English as an additional language

The good practice for supporting communication, language and literacy presented throughout this book applies equally to all children, including those learning English as an additional language (EAL). However, this chapter sets out to discuss some of the more specific issues relating to bilingualism and biliteracy, and looks at the practical implications of providing effective additional support for children who are learning in more than one language.

The foundations of good practice

For many children in the EYFS, English is not their first language at home. In some settings there may be several different languages represented. These children will all be at different stages of learning English; some may be bilingual or even multilingual. Whatever stage they are at, their first language is central to their identity and this should be recognized, respected and valued. Such linguistic diversity brings a huge richness to any learning community, and reflects multicultural Britain today. The environment of the setting should embrace this, not only through its resources, signs, books and displays, but also through the attitudes and understanding of the staff. The foundations for this are underpinned by three key principles.

1. The linguistic, social and psychological needs of EAL learners require both languages to be respected, valued and used in their learning

Long-established research (e.g. Cummins, 1994) and seminal projects such as the Multilingual Resources for Children Project (1995) continue to demonstrate that helping children to be confident in their own language gives them a firmer foundation upon which to build the learning of their second language. In other words, there are sound linguistic reasons for not excluding the home language from the educational setting. Recent research continues to confirm this theory, and emphasizes the impact of parental involvement (NAA 2008a). In line with the EYFS principles for all children, involving and consulting parents about the home language not only provides a valuable source of information but also promotes better understanding by those parents of their children's progress. Our language is part of our identity. To prevent or discourage children from using their home and community language can undermine their confidence and self-esteem. It could even imply that English is in some way superior, and tension between the two languages could lead to conflict and confusion. Alternatively, to demonstrate to children that their language is valued and respected can provide a positive approach to learning the two languages side by side.

2. The language learning needs of EAL children do not necessarily reflect their ability in other areas of the curriculum

It is sometimes wrongly assumed that a child who is in the early stages of learning English is also at a lower level of understanding in other areas of learning. EAL learners are not necessarily children with special educational needs or disabilities. Their levels of ability vary alongside all children and will represent the full range including high achievers and gifted and talented.

3. The linguistic, social and psychological needs of monolingual English speakers require a variety of languages to be respected, valued and used in their learning

Exploring the diversity of languages, accents and dialects, including Standard English, can help children to develop their knowledge and understanding of how language works, and is required by the National Curriculum. The multilingual setting offers a stimulating and interactive environment for learning not only about languages and texts but also about how to build mutually rewarding relationships between children from different cultural backgrounds. Such learning is important for all monolingual English-speaking children, regardless of the cultural ratios in their community.

Knowledge of languages

All adults working with EAL children have a responsibility to acquire a useful knowledge of their languages and cultures. This does not mean becoming fluent in all the languages you are likely to encounter! That would be unrealistic. But to learn some words and phrases, particularly greetings, gives a strong message that you are not only interested but also approving and accepting. Involving the child in teaching you and other children about their language is also a valuable way into discussions about language.

Other information you might need to obtain includes:

- Do both parents speak the same language?
- Is the home language also a community language?
- Is the spoken language the same as the written?
- In which direction does the written text travel?
- Is there a special language for the purposes of religion?
- Is the child educated by other educators (e.g. community language teachers)?

ACTIVITY 4.1 Finding out more about other languages and cultures

Before starting this activity you will need to consult with your workplace manager or trainer. Using a copy of Activity Sheet F, research a language and culture of your choice that is relevant to where you work or live. Try to talk to a parent about this to get their views on how the setting can best help their child and how barriers are overcome.

Why do EAL children need additional support?

Language exists in order for us to communicate with one another. Throughout this book, the integrated nature of language is discussed; the links between speaking, listening, reading and writing are a natural and constructive part of children's language learning. These processes are interactive and require exchanges with others. EAL children benefit enormously from working in English-speaking groups because it gives them opportunities to:

- listen to the sounds of English;
- observe the exchanges of others;
- practice their responses in English;
- ask questions;
- answer questions;
- repeat what they hear;
- use body language for clues;
- receive support from other children.

Working in a pair with a child who speaks the same home language offers EAL children opportunities to:

- consolidate ideas;
- clarify areas of uncertainty;
- answer questions;
- translate;
- develop confidence in their learning.

Working in a pair with a child who speaks English offers both children opportunities to:

- write dual texts;
- discuss and translate;
- listen to both languages;
- speak both languages;
- teach each other about their languages.

Working with an English-speaking supporting adult (Figure 4.1) offers EAL children opportunities to:

- share their worries;
- ask questions in English;
- answer questions in English;
- repeat and practice;
- revisit previous learning;
- talk about their home language;
- 'teach' the adult;
- enjoy looking at books;
- observe writing.

Figure 4.1 Support should be offered in the home language as well as English

Figure 4.2 Sharing dual-language books offers a rich source of discussion and interest

Working with a supporting adult who speaks the child's home language (Figure 4.2) offers that child opportunities to do all the things in the previous list plus:

- develop their home language;
- learn to switch between languages;
- listen to ideas explained in their own language;
- have instructions translated;
- answer questions in their own language;
- ask questions in their own language;
- conceptualize ideas in their own language.

Working on their own, EAL children have no opportunity to experiment, listen and respond. Isolated and passive learning situations are totally inappropriate to their need for dynamic interaction.

ACTIVITY 4.2 Bilingual group observations (Time: various 10-minute intervals)

Using Activity Sheet G, observe and compare different bilingual children. The sheet describes the observation process in more detail.

Examples of interactive activities

All babies and young children need to learn through interactive contexts across all areas of learning. They need to see, hear, touch and move. This is particularly important for EAL children because a multisensory approach to learning contributes to their cognitive and linguistic progress as well as making the learning fun. Here are some examples of the types of activities that are particularly useful to EAL learners:

Bookmaking   Storytelling and technology create an active learning situation in which children can talk, listen, write, read, make and draw.

Booktalk	Sharing picture-books enables the EAL child to listen, say and look. The pictures provide a strong context for the child to make meaning. Books with a repeated pattern are also useful for enjoyable practice, as are rhyming and rhythmic verse. Books that have a box of related artefacts are particularly useful. Making collections of items to illustrate or illustrate the story can also be fun for the children.
Storytelling	Telling known stories, new stories or stories about oneself – the ancient art of storytelling is central to human existence and is a completely cross-cultural activity, as natural as talk itself.
Retelling	In all areas of learning, the opportunity to retell reaps rich rewards for EAL learners. Artefacts can serve a useful purpose in reminding the child as he or she retells. These could range from the seeds which have just been planted to the clothes to be put on after PE.
Drama/role play	Playing the roles of others helps children to explore and experiment with a range of language for a variety of purposes.
Puppets	Designing and making puppets is fun, but to use them is even better. Links with storymaking and technology again make this a dynamic hands-on activity with a lot of purposeful communication.
Masks	A mask can help to give a child the confidence to speak because he or she has a shield. The child can also become someone else. Characters from stories can be a powerful voice for a child to use when developing confidence in spoken language.
Photographs	Photographs of the children, their families and other related subjects can be a tremendously stimulating resource for young children. They can be used for discussion, displays, art activities and bookmaking.
Cooking	Nothing motivates children quite like eating! Cooking and eating provides particularly good opportunities to explore cultural variety in an exciting and experiential way.
Visitors	A visitor focuses children's attention, whether that visitor is a newborn baby or the local vet. Listening and questioning have a real context when appropriate people visit an early years setting, and the activity provides an opportunity to broaden the variety of role models for the children.
Visits	Educational visits do not have to take all day and needn't cost anything. The local area will always provide a good range of resources to stimulate children's language and provide excellent starting points for learning by building on what the children know well.
Festivals	Festivals provide a starting point for a wide range of cross-curricular and discrete language development work.
Play	All play activities provide opportunities for language development. The talk that takes place during play can help children to organize their thoughts. Toys give children additional cues for their spoken language.
Writing area	A writing area that is resourced with a wide range of writing implements; different types, sizes, colours and shapes of paper; and displays of different types of texts can be very inviting to children if they are encouraged and rewarded for their efforts.
Listening area	Listening to story CDs with a book is a popular activity for all children. CDs can also be used for games, instructions and repeating an activity.
Computers	Programs with graphics and sounds are invaluable for EAL learners. Multimedia systems and interactive whiteboards are also valuable means of providing audio-visual enhancement of the learning.

Dual and alternative language books

Dual-language texts offer all children the opportunity to examine and learn about another language, while at the same time supporting children who are learning English as a second language (Figure 4.3). Indeed, dual-language texts can be used in a variety of valuable ways. However, they do vary in quality, so it is important for adults in early years settings to develop a critical awareness of these books in order to enhance their use and, where appropriate, influence purchasing decisions. The following questions are designed to help you focus your attention on a dual-language text in a way that critically evaluates the book.

- Which language comes first?
- Does one language have more prominence on the page?
- Are both languages written in the same size?
- Does each language have equal status?
- How has the inclusion of two texts affected the page layout?
- If one language is required to run in a different direction to English, what effect does this have on the reader?
- How will the book be read?
- Are the pictures useful to the reader?
- Is the author English?
- Is the story from the culture of the home language?

It is also appropriate to provide children with texts written in their home language only. Not only does this help to build the sound foundations of language and literacy in the home language, but it also helps to develop and maintain a sense of cultural ownership of those stories. To deprive children of stories and authors from their own cultures is to deprive them of a valuable part of their developing sense of self and can also affect their language development.

You will be reminded in Chapter 6 that there are many kinds of texts in addition to books. A print-rich environment in your setting should include resources, labels and displays that reflect the languages spoken. These not only support the learning of EAL, but can also be of great interest and value to all the children.

Figure 4.3 Dual-language labels help EAL children and are also interesting for all children

Developing a supportive relationship

Many of the qualities that you already offer when supporting children's learning will be particularly appropriate and helpful to EAL children. The following general principles can be applied regardless of the activity you have been asked to support.

- Remember that these children will know more about their language than you do.
- Tune in to what the children already know, including prior education.
- Take an interest in their language.
- Take an interest in their culture.
- Ask them to teach you some words.
- Try to link sounds to images.
- Use artefacts when explaining.
- Draw when explaining.
- Use artefacts when reading and telling stories.
- Make productive reference to pictures when looking at books.
- Include pictures in all writing activities.
- Use lots of body language to enhance meaning.
- Repeat what you have said often.
- Ask the children to repeat often what you have said.
- Ask the children to retell what others (e.g. the teacher) have said.
- Be a good listener.
- Learn from what you hear.
- Correct mistakes by being a role model rather than a critic.

Assessment

In Chapter 3, the importance of observation was explained and how this links to assessment and planning. The inclusion of another language in addition to English means that the assessments will have a broader focus for EAL children. It is important to distinguish between children's progress in their home language, their progress in English and their progress in the other areas of learning. Clear and specific guidance on this is available from NAA (2008b).

Assessing CLL

The first three points in all the scales can be assessed in the home language, but points 4–9 need to be assessed in English.

Assessing the other areas of learning

All the other scales across areas of learning, except CLL, can be assessed in the home language. Local authorities can be consulted for support with home languages in your area.

Assessing progress in the home language

An overall picture of the child's knowledge and understanding in their home language enables practitioners to plan appropriate play and learning activities. It is also important for parents to understand that this is a valuable part of helping the child make progress in their overall learning.

ACTIVITY 4.3 Assessing CLL   (Time: one hour)

Look at the EYFS assessment scales. Consider how the first three points on the CLL scales might be assessed in a child's home language. Now look at points 4–9 to understand why these need to be assessed in English.

EAL glossary

- **accent** – variation in pronunciation
- **dialect** – variations in grammatical structure/vocabulary
- **monolingual** – speaks in one language proficiently
- **bilingual** – regularly uses two languages to speak
- **biliterate** – able to read and write in two languages
- **multilingual** – speaks three or more languages (not necessarily proficient)
- **TEFL (teaching English as a foreign language)** – generally used in a non-English-speaking region
- **ESL (English as a second language)**
- **EAL (English as an additional language)** – provision for children whose first language is not English
- **TESOL (teaching English to speakers of other languages)** – usually applied to the teaching of adults within an English-speaking region

Notes for group leaders

Extending the listed activities

- Activity 4.1 – If different languages can be allocated to members of the group there will be scope for sharing and exchanging information, and even making a useful resource for future reference.

- Activity 4.2 – Discuss patterns and possible reasons for these. Compare EAL children with their English-speaking peers to see if there is a difference in the prominent types of talk used.

- Activity 4.3 – Looking at the *EYFS Profile Handbook* (QCA, 2008) together will prompt further discussion about the three types of assessment for EAL children.

Activities for assessment

- Case study of an EAL child to include observations, research into home language and culture, assessments, discussion with parent, examples of appropriate learning activities.

- Research the locations and ratios of different ethnic groups within the local authority and compare with the picture nationally. What provision is made to support the children of these groups?

Additional topics for group discussions

- What themes could stimulate ideas for puppet-making?
- Share ideas for collecting artefacts to extend a story.
- How might you design a role play area with dual-language texts?
- How would you go about making dual-language books?
- In what contexts might you make books with photographs and dual-language text?
- What is the value for all children of displaying dual-language labels and signs?

References and further reading

Baker, C. (2000) *The Care and Education of Young Bilinguals.* Bristol: Multilingual Matters.

Crosse, K. (2007) *Introducing English as an Additional Language to Young Children.* London: Paul Chapman Education.

Cummins, J. (1994) 'The acquisition of English as a second language', in Sprangen-Urbschat, K. and Pritchard, R. (eds) *Kids Come in All Languages.* New Delaware: International Reading Association, pp. 36–62.

DBS (1985) *Education for All* (The Swann Report). London: HMSO.

DCSF (2007) *Supporting Children Learning English as an Additional Language.* Norwich: DCSF Publications.

Edwards, V. (2009) *Learning to Be Literate: Multilingual Perspectives.* Bristol: Multilingual Matters.

McCardle, P. (ed.) (2007) *Childhood Bilingualism.* Bristol: Multilingual Matters.

Multilingual Resources for Children Project (1995) *Building Bridges: Multilingual Resources for Children.* Reading: Reading and Language Information Centre.

NAA (2008a) EAL Case Study, Islington: Reception Class Mother Tongue Project. London: QCA.

NAA (2008b) *Guidance Notes: Assessing Children who are Learning English as an Additional Language.* London: QCA.

QCA (2000) *A Language in Common. Assessing English as an Additional Language.* London: Qualifications and Curriculum Authority.

QCA (2008) *Early Years Foundation Stage Profile Handbook.* London: Qualifications and Curriculum Authority.

Thompson, L. (1999) *Young Bilingual Learners in Nursery Schools.* Bristol: Multilingual Matters.

Speaking, listening and thinking

This chapter explains how speaking and listening are an important and influential part of young children's learning, thinking and development. There is a brief introduction to the development of speech, followed by a discussion about the different types of talk for different purposes. It then goes on to discuss approaches to extending children's talk during the course of their daily learning. Good listening skills are also considered. This is put into the context of the EYFS framework and National Curriculum requirement followed by issues to be considered when planning talk activities.

Talk is central to our lives

Talk is central to all our means of communication in our everyday lives. It is the most significant difference between humans and other animals. Most of the time we take it for granted, unaware of just how important it is to our work, play and all the bits in between. Take a moment to think about how much talking you have done since you woke up this morning, even talking to yourself or listening to talk on the radio. Think about all the different people you have spoken and listened to, how many ways in which you have spoken and all the different reasons for your talk. Once we start to examine talk more closely we can begin to see that there are many different types of talk and that we talk in different ways for different purposes. We also adapt our talk according to the audience. For instance, you probably talk in quite a different way to your best friend than you do to your boss or teacher. The term 'oracy' is used to describe speaking and listening. It is the parallel word to 'literacy', used to describe reading and writing.

ACTIVITY 5.1 Analysing your own talk (Time: 15 minutes)

Using Activity Sheet H, record some of your own talk from yesterday. Start from a particular time of your choice, and retrace your movements from that point onwards as if you are replaying a DVD diary. Now analyse this more closely: consider who you were talking to and why, and how you were talking. Do you notice any changes? Is there any type of talk that was predominant? If you recorded your talk for another day of the week how might it be different?

Human talk is not only an amazing tool for direct, two-way communication, but it is also central to how we think, learn and socialize. Likewise, the texts that we read and write are constructed around the language that we speak. In other words, talk serves many different purposes in human communication. Figure 5.1 illustrates the key functions of talk. When working with babies and young children it is important to have a good awareness and understanding of these diverse functions of talk. This, in turn, helps us to recognize the importance of extending their talk at every opportunity in order to support these other aspects of their learning and development.

WHY IS TALK USEFUL?

- Talk communicates meaning.
- Talk communicates feelings and emotions.
- Talk communicates intention.
- Talk conveys instructions.
- Talk conveys responses to people and experiences.
- Talk can recall the past.
- Talk can predict the future.
- Talk reshapes and reinforces understanding.
- We answer questions through talk.
- We ask questions through talk.
- Talk allows the exploration and development of ideas by externalizing thought.
- Talk helps us to plan what we are going to write.
- Talk helps us to interpret what we are reading.

Figure 5.1 The key functions of talk

Learning to talk

From the moment they are born, babies make their feelings known through the sounds they make. Different types of crying signify different needs, and parents rapidly tune in to these in order to respond to what their baby is communicating. Random sounds, made with the tongue, lips and palate are known as babbling. These quickly become more focused as the baby realizes that they usually result in positive attention. The arrival of teeth extends the range of sounds further. When sounds resembling words are repeated back to the baby in their more accurate form, this provides positive reinforcement. Babies enjoy this rewarding socialization and the inevitable repetition provides a further form of teaching. As a result, recognizable words start to appear in the baby's vocabulary. Clusters of words emerge next, and eventually the structures of sentences are acquired. This dynamic interaction and learning demonstrates two vital factors in particular: the part played by the baby's own listening skills; and how greatly the baby's language development is influenced by the responses, reinforcement and modelling by those around them.

ACTIVITY 5.2 Interpreting the sounds made by babies (birth–11 months)

In consultation with your workplace, or by arranging a visit to a childcare setting for 0–3-year-olds, spend some time observing and noting down the variety of sounds made by a baby. Try to sort and code these. How many different sounds can you hear? Do some sound close to recognizable words? Do different sounds appear to have different meanings? Does the child listen to and imitate sounds made by adults? Do the sounds vary according to the social situation, for example when with other babies or just with an adult? If you have time, observe a second baby of a different age and compare your findings.

As young children develop, their language becomes increasingly sophisticated to accompany their developing thinking skills. Interaction with and modelling by adults continue to be significant contributing factors to children's rates of progress. Your work in an early years setting will mean that you have a great deal of influence on the language development of the children in your care. Your conversations, modelling, questioning, and teaching will all have an impact on each child's oracy. It is therefore crucial that you have a good knowledge of:

- different types of talk, so that you can extend the range and breadth of opportunities;
- how your own talk and interactions with children can have a positive impact on their oral development;
- how to ensure that children are also developing good listening skills.

Different types of talk

When working with babies and young children a good professional knowledge of the range of talk helps us to stimulate, support and extend children in the development of their speaking and listening skills. Here are some examples of the different types of talk that you may see young children using:

- telling stories;
- reciting rhymes and poems;
- reading aloud;
- exploring ideas;
- transforming ideas into firmer plans or decisions;
- predicting what might happen next;
- discussing;
- describing;
- explaining;
- justifying (opinions and actions);
- comments on the talk of others;
- role play;
- questioning;
- decision-making;
- expanding thought;
- evaluating;
- instructing.

Extending children's range of talk helps them to learn a wider range of grammatical structures and equips them with communication skills for different situations and purposes. However, they will not necessarily use these different structures automatically. The play-based learning opportunities and experiences that are provided should therefore be structured in ways that will encourage different types of talk. For example, if you want them to engage in **justifying** they will need an activity that will need justifying. A good example of this could be a sorting activity with an open-ended variety of solutions. A supportive adult might then be interested in why they resolved the problem in the way that they did. This might also be extended into predicting what might have happened if they had done the task differently. Such sophisticated language would include different tenses and vocabulary such as 'because', 'if', 'better', 'decided' and so on.

> **ACTIVITY 5.3 Encouraging different types of talk**
>
> This activity is designed to help you think about how you might promote different types of talk. Make a copy of Activity Sheet I and plan three activities that would encourage explaining, instructing and describing.

Extending children's talk

Every interaction in an early years setting is an opportunity for developing children's talk. For example, when they are tidying up they can be encouraged to think about how and why they are doing it in the way that they are. However, we cannot assume, just because talk is happening, that learning is taking place. On the contrary, there are many occasions where the talk might be limited and the interactions unproductive. Similarly, poor-quality input from adults can limit the learning and restrict the rate at which spoken language develops. So how can adults ensure that their input is making a valuable contribution towards extending children's oracy skills?

Responding and showing interest

If children feel that you value what they have to say they are more likely to talk. Following their interests is a good way to encourage talk, and asking questions that will encourage more complex talk, such as explanation, description and justification, can give the child a sense of importance because they are 'teaching' you.

Valuing and using the child's home language

Supporting children in the use of their home language, through gesture, visual cues and words and phrases they recognize, provides a vital scaffold to the development of their use of English. This enrichment and acceptance of the home language can positively support the learning of English alternatives.

Modelling

Children learn new language from what they hear so it is important that the adults around them model appropriate structures and vocabulary. They will learn new words from you only if you use and repeat them purposefully. They will imitate your structures if they hear them in meaningful contexts.

Interpreting and reframing

Correcting children's language needs to be done sensitively. Sharp reprimands can reduce confidence for some children and they could withdraw. Inferred criticism of incorrect language that might be used at home can also have a negative impact because a child's family network is the centre of their universe and at the core of their identity. Taking what a child has said and reframing it into the correct structure is a more supportive approach. For example:

'That cat is chasing the mouses.'
'Oh yes, he is, isn't he! He is chasing the mice. Why do you think he is chasing the mice?'

Commentary

Children's language can sometimes be supported by providing a commentary on what they are doing. 'Oh, I can see that you are mixing the colours. You have mixed red and blue! You have mixed them really well and now the colour has changed, hasn't it!'

Repetition and reinforcement

When learning new vocabulary and structures, we all need to hear them more than once. You will know this yourself if you have tried to learn a foreign language. Repetition can be found in stories, rhymes and songs, of course, but don't forget that children will need lots of opportunities to hear new language if they are going to use it confidently. This strengthens the learning so that it becomes established in their repertoire. When they start to use new phrases or words, your positive recognition and praise will also provide further reinforcement.

Questioning

Lots of questions will usually be heard in an early years setting. Children's own questions can lead to fruitful discussions for language development and this should be encouraged. Adult questions can vary in quality, however. Closed questions, those that require one correct answer, serve some purpose when checking specific knowledge, but can also limit the talk opportunities: for example, 'Is it hot or cold in the winter?' Open questions, those that lead to longer answers or a range of possible answers, open up the scope for more language to be used: for example, 'What sorts of things are different in the winter than in the summer?' Questioning is also a way of extending children's thinking, so don't always be satisfied with the first answer, but consider how your questioning might challenge the child's thinking and understanding even further. Questioning is also a significant component in the promotion of good listening skills.

ACTIVITY 5.4 Asking open-ended questions   (Time: 30 minutes)

Make a list of open-ended questions that you might ask across a range of activities with which you are familiar in an early years setting.

Promoting good listening skills

Some adults find it hard to listen; sometimes they hear the sounds without really listening. Children are just the same. The assumption is sometimes wrongly made that because children are sitting quietly on the classroom carpet they are listening well. Next time you are working with a child after a carpet session, how will you find out if he or she has been listening?

With skilled questioning and checking back, one can usually tune in to the level of listening that has taken place. However, when children cannot answer your questions, it is important to consider whether it is because they have not listened or because they have not understood. In actual fact they might have been daydreaming. This tuning out or switching off from the events around us is a highly developed safety mechanism that can sometimes be extremely useful when our brains are tired or in danger of overload. It can also be a habit that prevents children from listening and learning – a barrier to communication.

In order to help us understand why children tune out from listening, let us consider all the reasons why we, as adults, do the same thing. It might be because we are: tired; bored;

distracted; unable to understand the language; nervous; feeling outstripped by more talkative group members; unable to find the right words to express what we feel; afraid of being criticized; afraid of saying the wrong thing and making a fool of ourselves.

Can you think of any other reasons why you may become detached from a group situation? Taking the examples above, plus any additional ones of your own, can you match these to particular situations in which you have found yourself recently? Understanding the reasons why children are not listening can help us to plan strategies.

Listening skills need to be taught and this needs to be planned thoughtfully. Here are some of the listening skills that need to be considered so that opportunities to develop them can be included in the provision:

- listening and concentrating for increasing periods of time;
- listening to letter sounds in order to distinguish between them;
- listening in order to learn new words or structures, and extend language;
- listening in order to learn something new;
- listening to the answer to a question;
- retelling something that has been told;
- listening to another so that they can take turns to speak;
- listening to instructions so they can respond accordingly.

Speaking, listening and thinking in the EYFS

Helping children to develop good speaking and listening skills has always played a central role in good-quality early years provision. The EYFS framework emphasizes how important it is for children to have opportunities to learn, use and develop their speaking, listening and thinking skills as part of communication, language and literacy (CLL). It is covered in two aspects of CLL: 'Language for communication' and 'Language for thinking'. For assessment purposes, the two are linked together into one of the 13 nine-point scales described in Chapter 3 (p. 25). The early learning goals towards which children will be working are shown in Table 5.1.

Table 5.1 Early learning goals related to oracy (DCSF, 2008)

Language for communication

- Interact with others, negotiating plans and activities and taking turns in conversations.
- Enjoy listening to and using spoken and written language, and readily turn to it in their play and learning.
- Sustain attentive listening, responding to what they have heard with relevant comments, questions or action.
- Listen with enjoyment, and respond to stories, songs and other music, rhymes and poems and make up their own stories, songs, rhymes and poems.
- Extend their vocabulary, exploring the meanings and sounds of new words.
- Speak clearly and audibly with confidence and control and show awareness of the listener.

Language for thinking

- Use language to imagine and recreate roles and experiences.
- Use talk to organize, sequence and clarify thinking, ideas, feelings and events.

The EYFS provides good guidance on the types of age-related opportunities that might be provided to help children work towards these early learning goals, through effective practice, planning and resourcing. Note also that the earlier developmental matters for 'Linking sounds and letters' are also contributing to speaking and listening, although the actual early learning goals relate more closely to reading and writing. This emphasizes the point again that the strands of language are inextricably linked.

ACTIVITY 5.5 EYFS practice guidance   (Time: one hour)

Take time to familiarize yourself with the two sections of the EYFS relating to oracy in Table 5.1 by looking at 'Effective practice' and 'Planning and resourcing' in the practice guidance (DCSF, 2008).

Speaking and listening in the National Curriculum

The programme of learning for speaking and listening provides a framework for children to:

- develop essential knowledge, such as how language is expressed and information shared;
- learn key skills such as discussing and expressing viewpoints;
- use their knowledge and skills in other areas of the curriculum.

The breadth of learning should enable children to:

- develop and apply speaking and listening skills to suit a variety of audiences and purposes;
- tell and listen to stories and explore ideas and opinions in both formal and informal contexts;
- express themselves creatively in improvisation, role play and other drama activities;
- use digital and visual media to support communication both remotely and face-to-face.

Figure 5.2 Making and playing with puppets provides an excellent context for talk

If practitioners are to provide appropriate experiences to enable this essential knowledge and these key skills to develop, they need to understand the nature of talk and how it can be organised and managed. A good starting point for this is to develop an awareness of the different types of talk.

Planning for talk

Good early years provision should offer a balance of child-initiated and adult-led activities. When planning how this is to be delivered each day, it is necessary to consider what opportunities there will be for language development. Planning for oracy is essential if children are to make good progress in their language development. Figure 5.3 illustrates eight important aspects that should be considered when planning talk activities, whether they be adult interventions into spontaneous events or more focused approaches during taught activities.

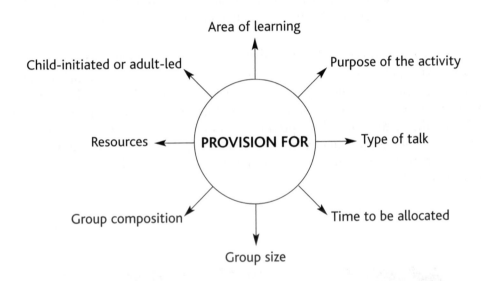

Figure 5.3 Things to consider when planning talk activities

1 **Child-initiated or adult-led**. Adult intervention and support for language will vary according to whether the activity is child-initiated or adult-led. Adult-led activities are easier in some ways because you can plan beforehand what language is being modelled, what questions are being asked etc. Child-initiated activities, on the other hand, are less predictable, and this highlights how important it is for you to be aware of the potential impact of any interventions you make.

2 **Area of learning**. Talk happens right across the curriculum range and opportunities for developing different types of talk can be identified in a clear and purposeful way.

Example: Creative development: predicting what will happen when colours are mixed.

3 **Purpose of the activity**. Children are far more likely to become involved in an activity if it has a clear and meaningful purpose.

Example: Physical development: child takes turns to give instructions to the next child about directionality.

4 **Type of talk**. If children are to develop a range of skills for communication through talking, it is important to ensure that they experience different types of talk.

Example: Guessing game = asking questions.

5 **Time to be allocated**. As with all activities, children will wander off-task very quickly if they are bored, struggling or have finished. However, children will always continue to talk. Sometimes it is appropriate to give a time limit for a task.

Example: Tell the other children about your painting = one minute for child to tell; two minutes for questions and comments from the others.

6 **Group size**. This will vary according to the activity but can certainly make a difference to the quality of input. Pairs work well. A trio can involve an observer/recorder dynamic. Groups of four tend to need more rules. Large-group discussions need very clear ground rules and these are best established in consultation with the children themselves. Too long in a large group situation can become frustrating for many children, hence the 'restlessness on the carpet' syndrome.

Example: Retelling a story = listen first, then tell the story to a partner.

7 **Group composition**. Self-selected friendship groups are sometimes appropriate, but occasionally it is valuable to place children with certain others. For example, it is sometimes appropriate to group all the vociferous children together, not just to give the others more of a chance but also to help the vocal children to practise their listening and social skills. Be aware of the effects that group composition has upon the quality of the talk.

Examples of combinations: Ability, mixed-ability, boys, girls, talkative, shy.

8 **Resources**. Merely being asked to talk is rarely enough to keep any group on-task for a sufficiently useful time. Talk tends to have a life of its own. This can be exciting and creative, but sometimes it can also mean that children are wandering off the learning focus into distracting and less productive interactions. Careful consideration of resources can enhance the quality of talk considerably and can help children to stay on-task. Resources are also an important means of ensuring that the children have something to talk about.

Figure 5.4 Using the telephone as a framework for talk

Notes for group leaders

Extending the listed activities

- Activity 5.2 with the group to see if there are any areas of commonality. This could be extended into a discussion about the developmental stages in the EYFS framework.
- Activity 5.4 – Discuss in pairs and give peer feedback on the quality of the questions.
- Activity 5.5 – Discuss the effective practice and share other examples that may have been carried out or observed.

Activities for assessment

- Activity 5.2 could be extended into a written assignment, supported by further research into the developmental stages.
- Activity 5.3 could be extended into a written assignment about how the activities were followed through and what were the outcomes. A critical evaluation would further strengthen this.
- Write a critical review of what research tells us about the links between children's spoken language and the development of their literacy skills.

Additional topics for group discussions

- Look at the *Practice Guidance for the Early Years Foundation Stage* (DCSF, 2008) to familiarize with the aspects outlined in this chapter. Share other actual examples of good practice that have been observed by group members (whole group).
- Look at the National Curriculum 'Understanding English, communication and languages' (QCDA, 2010) and discuss/share observations of activities you have observed in schools (whole group).
- Discuss when it is not appropriate to intervene in children's talk (whole group).
- Discuss the issues around 'correcting' children's speech (whole group).
- In groups of three, share ideas on how you might encourage certain types of talk in the following situations: water play, problem-solving, outdoor hunt for minibeasts.

References and further reading

Curran, M. (2007) *Speaking and Listening Games.* Dunstable: Brilliant Publications Ltd.

DCSF (2008) *Practice Guidance for the Early Years Foundation Stage.* London: DCSF Publications.

Evans, R. and Jones, D. (eds) (2008) *Metacognitive Approaches to Developing Oracy.* London: Routledge.

Holinger, P. and Doner, K. (2003) *What Babies Say before They Can Talk.* London: Simon and Schuster Ltd.

Jenkinson, R. (2004) *Learning to Talk.* London: Dorling Kindersley.

Preuss, M. (2005) *Talk, Listen, Think and Do.* Blackburn: Educational Printing Services Ltd.

QCDA (2010) *The Primary National Curriculum.* London: QCDA.

Sharp, E. (2005) *Learning through Talk in the Early Years.* London: Sage.

Reading from the start

This chapter explains the importance and complexity of the reading process. It aims to help you understand the different skills that children need in order to read, and how they develop as readers. It begins by asking you to focus on your own reading so that you can understand the various ways you tackle different kinds of text. This is explained further by examining the four categories of engagement with texts. How children learn to read is discussed, starting with babies, and this is then set into the context of the EYFS developmental framework. Government guidelines on the teaching of phonics are also introduced for you to follow up with further reading. A glossary of common terms relating to phonics is included at the end of the chapter.

The importance of reading

Reading is one of the first aspects of a child's education with which parents and carers are asked to get involved. Taking a book home each day to share or read together is common practice when the more formal teaching of reading starts in Key Stage 1. It is easy to see why reading has such an important place in our society. Not only does it support learning across the curriculum, right through to higher education, but it is also an important skill that is used every day by the majority of people. Books represent only one type of text that we read, as we live in a world that is packed with different types of print for a multitude of purposes. In fact, we are surrounded by text (see Figures 6.1, 6.2 and 6.3).

Figure 6.1 We are surrounded by text

Even if you don't often read fiction for pleasure yourself, just stop to think of the tremendous range of other texts that you read every day. It will become apparent to you just how significant reading is in your life.

Figure 6.2 Supermarkets are rich in print

Figure 6.3 Symbols are also contributing to children's concept of print

There are the texts that we actively seek out to read for the purposes of our work, our leisure and to perform many important operations within the running of our lives. Then there are the texts that confront us continuously in and around the environment. When we watch television we see text as well as pictures. We read a huge range of things on the internet and in emails and documents that people send us. And, of course, you probably read several text messages a day on your mobile phone. There is no doubt that reading is hugely important to our lives.

ACTIVITY 6.1 Texts that you have recently encountered   (Time: 10 minutes)

Think about some of the places you have visited during the past few days. This might include work, college, shops, bus station, train station, cinema or the doctor's waiting room. On a blank sheet of paper, jot down all the examples of text that you can remember from those situations.

Do we read everything in the same way?

Having identified examples of the texts that you encounter every day, let us consider how you read those texts. Imagine all the mail that might be delivered through your door on a typical day. The first envelope is your telephone bill. You know this before you have even opened it because of the type of envelope, the familiar logo and the way that it is addressed. Instantly, you have already used certain reading skills to make sense of this visual information. What do you do next when you have unfolded the paper inside the envelope? Do you start at the top left-hand corner and read systematically from left to right down the page until you have finished? Almost certainly the answer to this question will be 'no'. It is much more likely that you scan straight down to the total to see how much you owe. Now think about how you might read a menu in a restaurant. This can vary from person to person. Some may look at the wine list on the back page first so that they can enjoy a drink while choosing the meal. Others may look at the puddings first, or some may be looking just at the prices to spot the cheapest deal. This involves scanning to find different sections for different types of information. A train timetable involves quite complex cross-referencing, from station to station and between times, for instance, whereas a set of self-assembly instructions for your new bookshelves needs to be read systematically in sequential order. If you are reading a non-fiction book you are likely to refer to the contents page or the index first, whereas you are unlikely to read down the list of chapter titles of a romantic novel, unless, of course, you want some clues about the story in advance. In other words, we read different types of texts in different ways, and sometimes this requires different strategies or skills.

ACTIVITY 6.2 The texts that you read and how you read them　　　　　**(Time: 20 minutes)**

Using Activity Sheet J think carefully about the different types of texts listed. Next, taking each one in turn, try to recall exactly what you do when you read that type of text. This might include such things as where you start, how carefully you read it, the parts you ignore and the order in which you read it, how easily you recognize the words, etc.

By focusing on the different ways in which you read you will become more aware of just how complicated the reading process is. Young children have to develop a wide range of skills, knowledge and understanding about reading to enable them to take part effectively in this process. If you are going to support them in ways that will help them make good progress with reading, you should understand the important strategies that they will need to learn.

What strategies do we use when we read?

When you started to read this chapter how did you look at the text? Did you look at the individual letters and build up the sounds, taking each word separately to construct the sentences? Probably not. It is more likely that you recognized whole words and moved along the lines of writing in chunks. Speed readers are even able to read down the central column of a page taking in whole lines of text at once.

Experienced readers rarely need to 'sound out' the letters to build up a word as early readers do. They have developed the skills, understanding and knowledge to see and identify whole words as single units. However, if they encounter a strange word that they have not seen before (for example a foreign place name) they will probably need to go back to building up the letters into sounds, while at the same time drawing upon their knowledge of letter patterns from more familiar words that are similar in order to help with pronunciation and emphasis.

To help you experience how that works, here is a simple task. Look at the word below and try to say it out loud.

KNEBEVIGHT

You probably said something which sounded like 'neebvite'. Why did you not pronounce the K, the second E, and the G and H? You already know words with these silent letters and patterns in them and so you transferred the rules across. In other words you used your knowledge of letter shapes, letter sounds and spelling rules to say the word.

So you have read the word aloud, but have you really read it? No. All you have done is translated shapes into sounds. At the moment there is no meaning. Let us look at the word again in a sentence.

SALLY PULLED HER KNEBEVIGHT

How many possible meanings can you think of for this strange word? We know now that the word is a noun because of its relationship with the other words in the sentence. But is this in fact a sentence? Where is the full stop? Let's have some more clues.

SALLY PULLED HER KNEBEVIGHT ON

The addition of one more word makes an enormous difference to our understanding of the word, and yet still there is no clear meaning. Nor is there yet a full stop.

SALLY PULLED HER KNEBEVIGHT ON TO KEEP HERSELF WARM.

That narrows it down a bit, and yet, even so, the word could still have a variety of meanings – coat, hat, duvet... We have arrived at the end of the sentence because now we have a full stop. However, we still need more information in order to understand the meaning of our mystery word. If there was a picture we might be able to see what Sally was pulling on. In the absence of a picture, let us look further on in the text.

SHE LOVED THE FACT THAT IT MATCHED HER GLOVES.

Could the knebevight be her scarf? Read on.

AND SHE WAS GRATEFUL THAT IT WAS KEEPING HER HEAD WARM AND DRY FROM THE WIND AND SNOW.

I think we can be pretty sure now that the knebevight is a type of hat.

In order to make sense of Sally's story you had to:

- look at the graphemes (letter patterns) in the word;
- translate these into phonemes (sounds) by applying your knowledge of other words and spelling rules;
- connect the relationship of the words grammatically to decide whether it was a noun or a verb;
- use the context (meaning) for clues.

For the purposes of this very simple exercise these strategies took place one at a time because the text was revealed to you in parts. Under normal reading conditions the effective reader employs all those strategies almost simultaneously when encountering new words. An early reader, however, has not yet developed the skills to employ this range of strategies in such a sophisticated way. Learning to do this requires teaching, practice and experience of a range of texts and strategies.

Categories of engagement with the text

By now, you will have realized that when we read we employ different strategies to make sense of the text. Let us now look at these strategies more closely. The strategies that we use when we read fall into four categories illustrated in Figure 6.4.

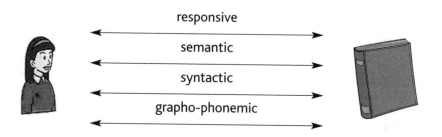

Figure 6.4 The four categories of engagement

The diagram represents the reader, the text and the four types of connection that take place between the two. These are called **categories of engagement** because they are pathways that 'engage' or 'connect' the reader in some way with the text.

1. Responsive engagement

This type of engagement is where the reader is responding to what he or she has read. At the very early levels of reading this might include a toddler pointing to a picture and laughing. At a more developed stage this could mean a child talking about why he or she does not like a certain character and predicting what is going to happen next. Response is more than understanding because it brings to the text the reader's own experiences and individuality.

2. Semantic engagement

Semantic engagement is the level at which the reader is making meaning from the text. It is about understanding what has been read. This involves getting clues from pictures, understanding the meanings of words and also how the words are organized, for example 'the cat was on the hat' means something different from 'the hat was on the cat'.

3. Syntactic engagement

The organization of words in a sentence is known as syntax. This is guided by grammatical rules and punctuation. Understanding these conventions helps the child to decipher and understand the text. For example, full stops give us important information to help us make sense of what we read.

4. Grapho-phonemic engagement

The 'graph' part means visual and the 'phon' part means sound. Quite simply, this aspect of reading is about seeing the shapes of the letters and transforming them into the sounds that make words. It is often referred to as 'decoding' the text. The glossary at the end of this chapter gives you further definitions of the main phonic terminology.

ACTIVIY 6.4 Thinking about the categories of engagement   **(Time: 10 minutes)**

Refer back to the notes you made during Activity 6.3 and try to allocate each of the strategies you used to one of the four categories of engagement.

By going through this process you will notice that there is overlap and interweaving between the categories of engagement. It is most important to remember that they work simultaneously when the reader is experienced. However, when children are in the early stages of learning to read, they are more likely to use strategies in isolation. For example, children may read in a 'robot voice' from their books without any errors and yet when they reach the end they do not remember what they have read. In other words, they have been decoding but not understanding. There are several important things to remember about the four categories of engagement:

- They are not learned in a special order one after the other.
- Individual readers will use them in different proportions.
- Some children need support within one category more than others.
- The effective reader uses them in combination.

Starting with babies

There are various programmes providing guidance on introducing babies to reading. Some multi-agency trusts, charities and local authorities provide parents with books as soon as their baby is born. This reflects the recognition that the early enjoyment of language, rhythm and rhyme gives a child a good foundation for learning to read. Babies are programmed to learn. They take an interest in everything around them and pictures and books are no exception. Hearing the structures of songs, nursery rhymes and the language of stories can capture their interest if it is a fun part of play and the close social interaction involved in sharing a book. This last point is an important one because the notion of 'teaching babies to read' could be misguided if it is seen as a formal and mechanical task. The emphasis should rather be on engaging with texts, enjoying the use of language, talking about pictures, predicting and joining in with sounds and rhymes, repeating favourite stories and, most importantly, adults reading *to* the baby for sheer pleasure. Such rich, varied and enjoyable experiences will be preparing the ground for their readiness and motivation to read at a later stage. They will know that reading is a fun thing to do and that print carries meaning.

Figure 6.5 Sharing books with babies lays important foundations for learning to read

The developing reader

Some years ago, early years teachers were trained to teach what were then called 'pre-reading' or 'reading readiness' skills. These included activities such as picture matching, listening, sight recognition and memory games and were provided in order to 'prepare' children for reading. During the 1950s children would only be given reading books once they knew enough letters and sounds to be able to decode those books.

Today, such games continue to be a useful part of children's learning, but the notion that this is 'pre-reading' has been rejected. Instead, it is recognized that reading skills develop on a continuum rather than the children reaching a point where suddenly they are readers when the day before they were not. For example, a three-year-old sharing a book with an adult might:

- talk about the story and point to the pictures;
- predict what might happen on the next page;
- join in with or fill in some of the missing words as a game.

When shopping they will take an interest in packaging and are likely to know what the writing represents; they may recognize signs and logos. This relationship with texts is an important stage of the child being well on their way to reading (and writing), even if they have not started to decode text. They are emerging as a reader. The emergent reader is the child who:

- knows what books are for;
- enjoys stories;
- can talk about books;
- recognizes that print is a code that represents words.

It is staggering how much knowledge young children can acquire about reading through other activities as well as sharing books. The word TESCO on a carrier bag, the STOP sign at the end of the road, the shopping list, the birthday card all carry particular messages that are understood by many young children. Earlier in this chapter you were asked to focus on the variety of print in your life. Such a rich and varied print environment has a profound effect on the early learning of young children and it should not be ignored, because it provides a stimulating and comprehensive basis for learning about how reading works.

As the child begins to learn more systematically about the components of reading (the letters, sounds, words and grammar), he or she begins to move towards becoming a supported reader. At this stage the child is showing an interest in tackling some print with the help of a more experienced reader. He or she will look at books for pleasure but needs help to read unfamiliar texts. At this point, they need more systematic high-quality phonics teaching to help them develop strong skills of decoding text and word recognition. This is a statutory requirement for all children in the EYFS, regardless of the type of setting, because it has been proven to make a real difference to children's competence in reading and writing (Rose, 2006).

Gradually the child develops into a fluent reader as he or she builds up a more complex knowledge of how texts work. The child will tend to revisit familiar texts that can be read with confidence, but also approach new texts with increasing skill and confidence. At this stage the child will start to read some parts of some texts silently.

Eventually the child will develop into an independent reader. Typically, a child at this stage will be choosing texts from a range of sources, will understand what is read and be able to discuss it with reference to the text. The child will also be starting to read 'between the lines' (inferential reading) for hidden or implied meanings.

This brief overview of the developing reader not only presents a continuum of learning from birth to five but also demonstrates how all strands of language learning are interlinked. Talking (e.g. playing rhyming games), listening (e.g. distinguishing the sounds in words) and writing (e.g. mark-making to reinforce letter recognition) all contribute to the process of learning to read.

Figure 6.5 Reading and writing are closely interlinked

Reading in the EYFS

The five strands of the EYFS statutory framework for 'Communication, Language and Literacy' (CLL) inevitably overlap, each one contributing in some way to children's development as readers. However, there are two strands that you should look at particularly. They are: 'Linking letters and sounds' and 'Reading'. The early learning goals are provided in Table 6.1 overleaf. The development towards these goals is described for each age band, supported by examples of effective practice, guidance on planning and resourcing, and what to look for when observing and assessing.

The 'Linking letters and sounds' strand is supported by a comprehensive package of phonics guidance and teaching resources, available free from the DCSF and also downloadable from their website. This follows a government review (Rose, 2006), which made strong recommendations for the systematic daily teaching of phonics. A simple model is provided as a framework for understanding how children learn to read. This presents two dimensions of reading: word recognition and language comprehension. The model of teaching works on the interplay between these two sets of processes. There is a clear and specific approach that needs to be followed under the statutory framework for phonics. It should be multisensory, time-limited and taught daily at a brisk pace at a dedicated special time. However, it is also recognized that there will be cross-curricular opportunities for developing phonological awareness at other times in addition to this discrete input. The need for careful assessment and monitoring is emphasized and knowledge of the detail is vital to your own professional knowledge. Comprehensive details of what should be taught can be found on the DCSF website and in the *Linking Letters and Sounds* pack (DCSF, 2007). Knowledge and understanding of this is essential for anyone who is supporting learning in the EYFS. The phonics glossary at the end of this chapter introduces you to the more common terminology that you will come across in early years settings and schools.

National Curriculum expectations for reading

The programme of learning for reading provides a framework for children to:

- develop essential knowledge, such as the power of language and communication to engage people and influence their ideas and actions;
- learn key skills such as evaluating or discussing what they have read;
- use their knowledge and skills in reading across other areas of the curriculum.

Table 6.1 Early learning goals related to reading development (DCSF, 2008)

Linking sounds and letters

- Hear and say sounds in words in the order in which they occur.

- Link sounds to letters, naming and sounding the letters of the alphabet.

- Use their phonic knowledge to write simple regular words and make phonetically plausible attempts at more complex words.

Reading

- Explore and experiment with sounds, words and texts.

- Retell narratives in the correct sequence, drawing on language patterns of stories.

- Read a range of familiar and common words and simple sentences independently.

- Know that print carries meaning and, in English, is read from left to right and top to bottom.

- Show an understanding of the elements of stories, such as main character, sequence of events and openings, and how information can be found in non-fiction texts to answer questions about where, who, why and how.

The breadth of learning should enable children to:

- read widely for pleasure;
- develop their reading skills to become critical readers;
- engage with a wide range of texts (including media texts);
- work with writers of all kinds in and beyond the classroom.

More detail of how the curriculum for reading should progress and the levels that children are expected to reach can be found on the QCDA website (www.curriculum.qcda.gov.uk).

Phonics glossary

- **to blend** – to build up and combine individual sounds together to pronounce a word, e.g. s-t-o-p, blended together, reads 'stop'
- **cluster** – where more than one letter makes more than one sound when combined, e.g. in the word 'traffic' there are three sounds represented by the first three letters
- **CVC words** – consonant-vowel-consonant words such as 'cat', 'mop' and 'rip'
- **decoding text** – translating the visual shapes of the letters into sounds in order to say the word (from graphemes to phonemes to word)
- **digraph** – where two letters combine to make a third new sound, for example:
  - sh, ch, th, ph are consonant digraphs
  - ai, oo, ow are vowel digraphs
  - the a and e in 'plate' are a split digraph because another letter separates them
- **grapheme** – what a sound looks like, i.e. the letter or letters used to represent it, for example the sound 'oooo' can be represented using four different graphemes in these words – 'chew', 'blue', 'through' and 'too'
- **phoneme** – the smallest unit of sound, for example 'cat' has three separate sounds represented by three letters, whereas 'shop' also has three sounds even though there are four letters
- **to segment** – to break up or 'sound out a word into its separate sounds (phonemes) in order to spell it
- **whole-word recognition** – seeing the whole shape of the word and saying it rather than having to sound it out by decoding the letters into sounds

Notes for group leaders

Extending the listed activities

- Activity 6.1 – This can be carried out as a whole-group task.
- Activity 6.2 – In pairs, sort the examples into 'types' of reading. Do any patterns emerge across the larger group?
- Activity 6.3 – This will be greatly enhanced by further discussion about the strategies that are used for each text. Ask them what knowledge they already had to draw on in order to decode and interpret the texts. Look at the simple reading model in *Linking Letters and Sounds* (DCSF, 2007) and discuss which texts required word recognition and which drew on language comprehension.

Activities for assessment

- Activity 6.4 could be developed into a more in-depth written analysis.
- Select five children's books that reflect different levels of reading development. Write a summary of each, including the text level, structure, use of pictures, complexity of storyline etc., then explain how this might be suitable for children at a certain level of reading development.
- Make a collection of books for babies and write about how you would use them; for example, by using extended actions, games and rhymes.

Additional topics for group discussions

- Discuss and share ideas for rhyming games with actions that might be used with babies.
- Look at the detail in the *Linking Letters and Sounds* pack or on the DCSF website. Discuss the principles of high-quality phonic work.
- In groups of three, make a collection of examples of print that are not on paper, and make a display.
- In groups of four, share ideas for linking reading and writing with three-year-olds.

References and further reading

Browne, A. (1998) *Teaching Reading in the Early Years.* London: Sage.

Bruce, T. and Spratt, J. (2008) *Essentials of Literacy from 0–7 Years.* London: Sage.

Campbell, R. (2009) *Reading Stories with Young Children.* Stoke-on-Trent: Trentham Books.

Davies, A. (2010) *Reading to Your Baby.* London: Carroll & Brown Publishers.

DCSF (2007) *Linking Letters and Sounds: Principles and Practice of High Quality Phonics.* London: DCSF Publications.

DCSF (2008) *Practice Guidance for the Early Years Foundation Stage.* London: DCSF Publications.

Evans, J. (2009) *Talking beyond the Page.* London: Routledge.

Gooch, K. and Lambirth, A. (2008) *Understanding Phonics and the Teaching of Reading: Critical Perspectives.* Milton Keynes: Open University Press.

Rose, J. (2006) *Independent Review of the Teaching of Early Reading.* London: DfES.

CHAPTER 7

Supporting children's reading

In the previous chapter we looked at reading processes and strategies. This chapter goes on to link that theoretical knowledge to the everyday practicalities of working with babies and young children. It begins by emphasizing the importance of relationship skills when supporting children with their reading. It looks at how you might work with individual children to support their reading, and also describes the different group approaches commonly found in early years settings and Reception classes. Additional support for children who find reading difficult is discussed. The value of reading games is explained, with some ideas about making your own games to link with popular stories. Finally, reading is discussed within the context of role play and the other areas of learning.

Developing a supportive relationship

Those who work in early years settings spend much of their time supporting children's reading across a wide range of activities. Playing action games, enjoying rhymes, songs and stories, reading labels in the role play area, hunting for letters in the shaving foam and reading stories together are just a few examples of activities that contribute to children's developing skills as readers. As well as the quality of the activities, the quality of the relationships between children and supporting adults has a significant impact on the learning. Not only can this influence the development of a child's reading but it can also affect how the child perceives him/herself as a reader.

To begin, let us focus on what we mean by 'support'. Figure 7.1 illustrates four key qualities that you might bring to supporting children's reading.

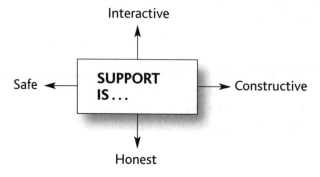

Figure 7.1 Components of support

These four components encompass all the important qualities required to support children with their reading. Let us look at each in turn.

1. Support is interactive

You are a valuable resource for learning, but advice, guidance and information can be offered in many different ways. It is therefore important that you do not think of yourself as a 'knowledge machine'. The support needs to be a two-way process so that you and the child are responding to each other. Ask yourself the following questions:

- How can I find out what the child needs to know?
- How can the child be encouraged to ask questions?
- How can the child learn from my example?
- How does the child perceive my explanations?
- How can I check that the child understands what has been discussed?
- How can I be a good reading role model?
- Do I leave enough space for the child to respond?

2. Support is constructive

A constructive approach to learning means building on what is already there in a positive and developmental way. We need to show respect for what the child can offer. When children share their ideas and expertise with an adult they are placing great trust in that adult. For some children this can be quite difficult because they feel they are exposing themselves to criticism, particularly when they do not get much support at home. If we start from the sound base of a child's current expertise we can always find a positive focus. Children respond more effectively to praise than criticism, and building on their expertise has the additional benefit of boosting their self-esteem. Questions for you to consider include:

- Am I respectful towards the child, showing that I value what they already know and can do before correcting them? Or do I always 'pounce' immediately on the mistakes?
- If so, what impact does this have on the child?
- Am I aware of individual differences between children's abilities and needs?
- How can I identify what the child is already doing well?
- How can I praise sincerely and specifically so that the praise adds to the learning?
- How can I offer constructive feedback for improvement?
- How can I encourage the child to contribute to that evaluation process and identify for themselves what the next steps for improvement might be?
- Do I give children the opportunity to revisit and practise the areas for improvement?

3. Support is honest

Honesty is important in any relationship. Children soon know if an adult is patronizing them or giving praise where praise is not due. Being honest in the reading relationship is not necessarily about pointing out all the mistakes, but it can be about the following:

- correcting a realistic number of errors in a constructive way;
- praising specifics rather than making general statements;
- giving your own opinions about the book you are sharing;
- disagreeing with the child in an OK way;

- allowing the child to disagree with you in an OK way;
- giving positive feedback before identifying areas for development;
- asking the child for his or her opinions;
- encouraging children to be honest with each other;
- talking about your own mistakes;
- talking about the books you read at home.

4. Support is safe

If children are going to try their best and are determined to succeed, they have to take risks with their learning. If they are afraid to try an unknown word because they are worried they might get it wrong, their learning will be held back. However, if they trust the adults with whom they work they will be more likely to experiment and explore. This means they will be pushing the boundaries of their learning, and this will lead to better achievements. Examples of this might include the books they choose, the ideas they express, disagreeing with your opinions about books, asking questions, setting their own targets and so on. Now ask yourself the following:

- How do I show children that I respect their expertise?
- Do I encourage children to take risks (e.g. have a go at a strange word)?
- Do I ensure that children are comfortable?
- Do I give children the time they need?
- Do I provide opportunities for children to discuss their own learning?
- Do I provide opportunities for children to set and review their own targets?
- How do I show children that I value their efforts?

ACTIVITY 7.1 Self-evaluation exercise   **(Time: 15 minutes)**

Evaluate your own practice against the four areas that have just been described. Use the questions to help you. Don't be afraid to be accurate and honest. We need to know where our weaknesses lie in order to do better. Write down the things you do well, and choose three things that you would like to try to do better. If possible, discuss these with your group leader or manager.

Supporting individual reading

Parents are often asked to hear their children read at home. In Reception classes, working with individual readers is a common requirement of learning assistants. However, there is sometimes a danger that this can become a regimented chore when a list of children has to be completed, and the children are merely passing through a production line. For the child, this is an important time and a time that deserves quality input from you. It is worth remembering that each child may bring to this experience a different attitude. Here are some examples:

'Oh, good! It's my turn!'

'Oh, no! It's my turn!'

'Why does she always want me to read to her when I'm in the middle of playing?'

'I'm frightened that I may get it wrong.'

'I'm no good at reading...'

Can you think of any more examples? The child's attitude will be influenced, to a large extent, by their previous experience of reading with you. In other words, if you were impatient with the child for mispronouncing words yesterday, he or she is unlikely to feel very enthusiastic about repeating the process today.

There are three questions that you need to consider when working with individual readers. How can you ensure that the experience is enjoyable? How can you ensure that the child is learning more about reading during this time? How can you report back information that will be useful to the teacher?

Ensuring that the experience is enjoyable for the child

Putting children at their ease is not merely about being a kind and caring person; it is about creating an atmosphere in which children want to learn and feel motivated to work to their optimum ability.

- Be sensitive in your timing.
- Try to invite, rather than demand, the child to share a book with you.
- Put the child at ease and make it fun.
- Discuss the book he or she has chosen to read before asking them to read it. Look at the cover. Try to predict what is going to happen. Recall what has been read before.
- Do not rush the child – leave time for self-correction.
- Respond to what the child is doing well and be encouraging.

Ensuring that the experience is a valuable learning time for the child

Part of the skill of extending children's learning is to target an appropriate learning objective. What do they already know? What do they need to learn next? How can they best achieve that? However, if you attempted to do all the things listed below, the child would hardly find time to read! Consider carefully, in consultation with the teacher, what the child can already do in order to identify which of the interventions below are appropriate. Interrupting the flow can be unproductive and frustrating for the child; it may distract them or interrupt their concentration, so knowing when to step in is a skill that you should be aware of.

- Let the child hold the book and turn the pages, even if you are doing the reading.
- Talk together about the book features (cover, front, back and author).
- Talk together about the pictures.
- Talk together about the characters.
- Talk together about the language features (letters, words, spaces etc.).
- Talk together about the child's own experience that may relate to the story (e.g. the child's own pet if the story is about a dog).
- Encourage the child to look for clues when reading.
- Encourage the child to build up the sounds of words.
- Encourage the child to read for meaning in sections (discuss as you go).
- Allow time to revisit or read again any areas of uncertainty.
- Read along with the child in unison if he or she needs support.
- Where you are doing all the reading, encourage the child to predict or guess some of the words as you read.
- Encourage the child to predict and explain.
- Praise specific strategies rather than just saying 'Very good!' (e.g. 'I liked the way you chopped up that word to help you work it out!').

Observing and assessing

If you spend a period of quality learning time with any one child you are bound to collect vital information that will prove useful to the teacher (see Chapter 3). When working with reading, try to consider the following points in particular when reporting back your observations and assessment information.

- Make your comments informative. 'Jason read nicely' tells the teacher nothing of value. Does this mean that Jason read fluently, understood what he read, read with expression or read new words? A comment such as 'Jason is starting to refer back to the start of the sentence again to find clues to the meaning when he gets stuck on a word' is far more useful.

- The mistakes that children make when they are reading can be a useful means of identifying the strategies or phonic knowledge that need further teaching. Try to note these down if there is an obvious pattern. For example, 'Sameena is decoding the start and middle of the word but is not looking to the final sound in CVC words.'

- Take note of the child's attitude towards reading and books. Are they enjoying, struggling, reluctant, preferring non-fiction, anxious, confident etc?

Information such as this will help the teacher to provide relevant experiences and teaching that will target the gaps in the child's learning.

ACTIVITY 7.2 Getting to know a reader (Time: 40 minutes)

Please check with the teacher or manager before doing this activity. Make a copy of Activity Sheet L and arrange to share a book with the child that you and the teacher have chosen. Try to make this part of your usual routine so that the child feels comfortable. If writing in reading record books is part of the normal practice then it should be all right to jot notes down during the activity. You may wish to carry out this task several times with different children so that you can make useful comparisons.

Paired reading

Paired reading was developed in the 1970s and refers to a specific type of reading approach. It is a useful partnership that is designed to build children's confidence and fluency. The child and adult usually read simultaneously, although the child is usually fractionally

Figure 7.2 Children love looking at photos and these can be used to make interesting books for shared reading

behind. However, if the child wishes to read alone or would like the adult to read without them, they can request this by giving an agreed signal. The significant feature of paired reading is that the child is in control and can decide who reads and when. The signal can be part of the fun (e.g. tapping the back of the hand or nudging elbows) so that the experience is more like a game. Putting the child in charge like this can be less intimidating for those who lack confidence with their reading. The adult is there to provide support as and when the child needs it.

Shared reading

The approach known as shared reading has been adapted and honed over the years, particularly as more specific frameworks for teaching reading have been introduced by the government. The accepted understanding of the term now is that shared reading is used to extend children's learning beyond their current levels by teaching about how texts work through demonstration using a shared text. This is usually a large text such as a 'big book', poster or interactive whiteboards (IWB) so that everyone can see the text clearly. The teaching focus will be a reading-related aspect, with the teacher modelling and demonstrating to the group or class. For example, it might relate to phonics such as decoding by looking at specific letters and sounds; it might be about key features of a type of text, for example the use of contents and indexes in non-fiction books; or it could be about interpreting texts, for example reading and discussing a poem together. Discussing the features, pictures, characters, action, or author's style, or predicting, explaining, questioning, empathizing, comparing etc., all enrich children's understanding of and responses to texts. Clearly, there can be obvious links to writing at the same time, so the shared reading could be an introduction to a writing activity that then follows.

Figure 7.3 Children benefit from talking about what they are reading

Guided reading

This is an approach often used in primary schools where the teacher will work with a group of two to six children who are all at a similar level of ability for reading. They will each have a copy of the same book and will follow the print together, while taking turns to read aloud. The teacher will intervene from time to time to ask questions or teach a specific point. The teaching may relate to phonics (decoding), textual features, or comprehension according to the needs of the group. There will normally be a specific learning objective for the session and the teacher begins by sharing this with the children and introducing the book. The group may look at the book generally first, possibly discussing difficult words that they will encounter, thus preparing them in advance. This is also an opportunity for the teacher to observe which strategies each child is using in order to plan and refine ongoing teaching.

Reading games

Reading games are not only an enjoyable activity for children; they can also be an effective resource for learning. Reading skills and strategies can be placed within the context of a game to provide an opportunity to repeat, revisit and practise in ways that are motivating and meaningful.

Many types of games are commercially available, but it is also possible to make your own games. During a training course for teaching assistants at Oxford Brookes University trainees were asked to make a reading game using early years fiction as a starting point and theme. The design, making and evaluation of the game constituted one of the assignments for their course. The ideas they came up with were inspirational. They included game boards (*Rosie's Walk* by Pat Hutchins), cloze procedure (*We're Going on a Bear Hunt* by Michael Rosen), matching (*Dear Zoo* by Rod Campbell), sorting, rhyming snap (*Each Peach Pear Plum* by J. and A. Ahlberg), sentence-making (*The Snowman* by Raymond Briggs) and many more (Figure 7.4).

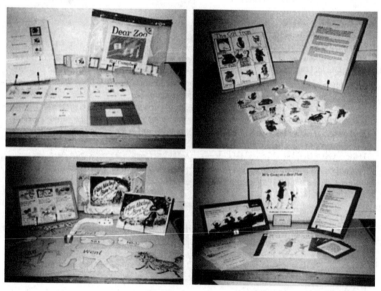

Figure 7.4 These reading games, using picture-books as starting points, were made by trainee teaching assistants at Oxford Brookes University

Trialling the games with groups of children was also an exciting part of this work. The enjoyment and learning was evident, and they were able to make adjustments to their games based on observations of how they worked in practice.

Using stories as starting points for games has many benefits. The game can be planned to introduce and use specific skills, but in addition, there are golden opportunities for talking about the book, characters, plot, author and so on. Games relating to specific books encourage children to use the language of those books and contribute to the literary environment.

ACTIVITY 7.3 Making and evaluating a reading game　　　　　　　(Time: 6 hours)

Part 1 – Making a reading game

Using children's literature as a starting point for activities in the classroom is just one way of enriching the literary environment in schools. Bearing this in mind, you are recommended to make a reading game that is based upon a picture-book. It can take any form you wish – e.g. board game, card game, tape etc. Think carefully about which specific aspects of reading the game addresses. Try to imagine the processes that a child will go through as he or she plays the game. These may not be the same as adult processes. It would be wise to include an instruction card in the game so that other adults will understand how to use it.

Try to ensure that any text and pictures within the game are clear and professionally reproduced. You may wish to use word processing for this rather than handwritten print. If you are able to laminate the game it is likely to last considerably longer than if it is used in its unprotected form.

Part 2 – Evaluating your game

This is not a set of instructions on how to play the game, but an explanation and justification of the methods employed. How is the game going to support the children who play it? What skills is it helping to develop? You may wish to support your explanations with references to background reading. Ideally, you will be able to show this to your teacher or group leader in order to receive some feedback. If this is not possible, it is nevertheless a useful process to evaluate your work for yourself. Perhaps you could exchange feedback with a fellow assistant who would also like to try this activity. The following questions might help you to do this:

- Does the game teach specific reading skills?
- Have I demonstrated a good understanding of those skills through the design?
- Are the playing instructions clear for children?
- Is the game well made and attractively presented?
- Have I learned from my observations of children playing the game?
- Can I adjust the game according to those observations?

Reading and role play

When children are role playing, they can be exploring, learning, practising and extending a whole range of skills and concepts. The learning that takes place during role play can depend very much on the quality of the provision. The support comes in the form of play materials and resources, but also in the form of adult intervention, even if the initial play is not adult-led. When children are playing independently in a role play area, they can sometimes benefit from occasional prompts from adults to model language and encourage reading and writing. We have already considered how resources might be provided in other areas of learning to encourage children to read. Let us now focus on your interventions into child-initiated role play by asking several questions:

- Do you ever go into role to join the child's fantasy?
- How do you draw attention to print within the role play area?
- How do you model yourself as a reader?
- How do you respond if the child 'pretend' reads?
- How do you respond if the child just 'reads' the illustrations?

- What sorts of questions do you ask children when they are role playing?
- Why is it sometimes better to observe from a distance during role play?
- Do you sometimes provide additional playthings to cater for unexpected developments?
- How do you show the children that role play is a worthwhile activity?
- How do you extend the role play into other activities?

Role play areas provide wonderful opportunities for children to extend their understanding of reading through play. It is very easy to collect a whole range of cost-free texts from all kinds of places to use for this purpose. For example: shops, garages, doctors and dentists, tourist information centres, hotels and restaurants, garden centres and used magazines and newspapers can provide a rich supply of leaflets, menus, brochures, catalogues, posters, display materials, window-dressing materials, scrap paper, carrier bags, bills, receipts, order pads, empty packaging, advertisements, food labels and boxes.

Not only can these resources be used to create a bright and stimulating role play environment, but they can also be used as resources for actual learning. They can be used in many ways to encourage the children to play, read and explore texts. Mail order catalogues, for instance, can really motivate children to use an index. Using laundry liquid bottles for measuring liquids can also provide opportunities to look at phonemes and words on the labels.

Children who find reading difficult

Assistants are often asked to work with children who are struggling with their reading. It is crucial to give all children a secure start with reading before they start in Key Stage 2 because teaching and learning from that point depend increasingly on reading for the other areas of the curriculum. This means that children who are behind with their reading can have problems in other subject areas as well. If they are not supported early enough they can often fall further behind. Clearly, you will be guided by the teachers with whom you are working. However, there are clear principles that will help you when you work with children who are below the usual expectations for reading.

Role of adult.

- **Praise and encouragement**. This doesn't just help them to feel happier, it can also be an effective way of reinforcing their learning. 'Well done, you remembered the sound that c and h make when they are together. What was that sound again?'
- **Bite-sized chunks**. Too much too soon can be overwhelming for children, particularly if they are feeling insecure about being behind. Give them challenges that are within realistic reach while also moving them on a step. This allows success and a sense of achievement. Slow progress is better than refusal or reluctance due to fear of failure.
- **Build on what they already know**. Hopefully, your tasks will be based on diagnostic assessment of what they need to learn next. Teaching children what they already know or something too far advanced is wasting their time and yours.
- **Make time for revision**. If you work with children such as these on a regular basis, always recap on the previous session before starting something new. These children often need repetition and revision.
- **Talk about reading**. Very often, these children have a fixed idea that reading is just about fiction. Help them to broaden their understanding by showing them and talking about other texts, e.g. comics, food packets, TV guides, football programmes etc.

Reading across other areas of learning

Some reading activities that take place in early years settings, particularly phonics, are discrete. In other words, they are separate and specifically about language and literacy. However, there are also opportunities for reading to be developed in the other five areas of learning. The following examples are provided here to help you identify opportunities for extending and supporting children's reading throughout the day.

Personal, social and emotional development	snack-time labels life stories family photos and labels
Problem-solving, reasoning and numeracy	stories reflecting a range of cultures matching shapes sorting and counting letters number stories counting books
Knowledge and understanding of the world	labels on displays talk about photographs look at old books use of non-fiction books directionality catalogues of home furnishings spelling games on the computer interactive stories on the computer religious books and stories stories from other cultures
Creative development	directionality shape and letter patterns pop-up books puppets rhythm and rhyme sounds and listening games
Physical development	fine motor skills – making letters movements of characters from books journeys and explorations from books treasure hunts outdoors

Don't forget that reading stories aloud is not the only activity that will enable you to support children's reading. The discussing, explaining, comparing, repeating and matching are equally valuable with non-fiction texts across the curriculum; and always be on the lookout for opportunities to draw children's attention to other types of texts. This can make a significant difference to the continued development of their reading skills.

ACTIVITY 7.4 Reading opportunities in other areas of learning   (Time: 30 minutes)

If you have never worked in a nursery it might be a good idea to arrange a visit before attempting this next activity. Look carefully at all the different learning experiences listed on Activity Sheet M and make notes about your ideas for developing certain aspects of reading during those activities. These might relate to an interest in books, awareness of print or recognition of letters or words. How might you extend the interventions you make with children in order to build on every opportunity for learning?

Many of the situations and activities described in this chapter may already have been familiar to you. Working with individuals or small groups to help their reading is perhaps the most common area of support for assistants to provide. However, this chapter has also aimed to emphasize that almost every minute of the day provides excellent opportunities for developing children's reading in a wide variety of ways. These are in addition to the planned discrete teaching of phonics and other reading activities. Labels on coat hooks and drawers, writing on displays, lists of words relating to topics, weather charts, registers, names and titles on workbooks, and so on, all provide ongoing opportunities for children to use and explore print. Drawing attention to texts, phoneme and word recognition, reading for a purpose, book talk and the sheer pleasure of stories and books all help to develop young children's reading strategies while at the same time giving them the implicit message that we regard them already as readers, that we respect their expertise and that we are firmly committed to extending that learning and development whenever we can.

Notes for group leaders

- Hold a discussion about the effective practice (EYFS) for supporting the reading development of babies to 11 months.

- Display the games from Activity 7.3 for the whole group to see. Evaluate each other's games in pairs and give feedback.

- Discuss the issues listed within the four categories of support.

- In groups of six discuss experiences of hearing children read. Who? When? How long? How often? Recording? Individual differences, and so on.

- In groups of three look at a picture-book, then collect ideas for follow-up activities across the curriculum.

- In groups of four discuss ideas for different role play corners and reading resources that could be provided for each.

References and further reading

Brock, A. and Rankin, C. (2008) *Communication, Language and Literacy from Birth to Five*. London: Sage.

Davies, A. (2010) *Reading to Your Baby*. London: Carroll & Brown.

DCSF (2008) *Practice Guidance for the Early Years Foundation Stage*. London: DCSF Publications.

Drifte, C. (2003) *Literacy Play for the Early Years: Learning through Non-Fiction*. London: David Fulton Publishers.

Harries, J. (2009) *Play in the EYFS: Role Play*. Dinton: Step Forward Publishing Ltd.

Mallett, M. (2003) *Early Years Non-Fiction*. London: Routledge.

Moyles, J. (2007) *Early Years Foundations: Meeting the Challenge*. Milton Keynes: Open University Press.

The developing writer

This chapter discusses the developmental nature of writing and how the experiences in early years settings can build usefully upon the early learning that has already taken place at home. It explains developmental models of writing and the actual processes of writing. The links across the CLL strands within the EYFS are re-emphasized, including the centrality of phonics. Spelling and handwriting are discussed and provision for teaching children to write is set into the context of play across the areas of learning. This includes writing on computers and collaborative writing. Ways in which you might support children across all these activities are woven throughout.

How does writing develop?

Throughout this book, reference has been made to the vital links between all the strands of communication, language and literacy: thinking, speaking, listening, reading and writing. Much of what has been said in Chapters 5, 6 and 7 also applies to the development of writing. As babies listen to and respond to different sounds, enjoy rhythmic stories and songs and start to distinguish sounds into words then phrases, they are learning about how language works. This absorption of the structures of spoken language are the early building blocks of written language. Likewise, as they develop fine motor skills through increasingly controlled manipulation, they are learning to take control of mark-making. They will start to make connections between the stories they enjoy sharing and the marks on the page. These complex processes are all working together to move the child through the journey towards becoming a writer. In childcare settings with provision for babies, a comprehensive range of stimulating and interactive learning experiences will support those processes. This will be contributing to the child's developing writing skills.

Young children joining early years settings have already accumulated a wealth of knowledge and understanding of the ways language works. They will be familiar with print within the social environment and many, though by no means all, will have had considerable experience of stories and books. In addition, they may have experimented with writing and sometimes regard themselves as writers within their own world of play. Basic concepts acquired are likely to include:

- print carries meaning;
- print is different from pictures;
- the words we say can be encoded into print;

- print can be spoken out loud;
- print written in English moves across the page from left to right;
- print is composed of different units – letters, words, spaces, sentences, etc.;
- print comes in different shapes, colours and sizes;
- writing is a meaningful activity;
- adults write for many reasons;
- adults read what other adults write.

These concepts provide the foundations for learning about writing. It is therefore important to recognize and value the education that has already taken place previously, both at home and in other settings. We must also acknowledge that children will be at different stages of writing development, regardless of age. Some will write fluently and confidently, some will write their own name, some will be unable to distinguish numbers from letters and so on.

Adults working with young children need to understand the developmental framework within which writing grows and changes. Approaches to writing that take this into account provide *continuity* for the child rather than presenting the child with a new and strange set of experiences that have nothing to build on.

There have been various influential models to demonstrate the stages of development in children's writing. In particular, Marie Clay (1975), through her careful and systematic observations of children's early writing, identified certain features that appear to be common to very young children (Figures 8.1–8.5). As with most developmental models, it is important not to regard such stages as independent units. There will always be overlap between phases as one merges into the other. However, what such models of developmental writing do help us with is the understanding that writing progresses – it changes. And those changes take place in a recognizable and sequential order. Recognition of the sequence enables us to define what the child has already learned and where he or she should be moving to next.

In Chapter 6, we looked at a model of reading in which the child moves from a supported role into independence. That same model is sometimes applied to writing, and is known as a 'developmental writing model'. The stages of **emergent → supported → fluent → independent** have been one useful way of regarding the developmental flow of writing, and the recognition of the early concepts mentioned at the beginning of this chapter are encompassed within the term 'emergent writer'. Children's perceptions of themselves as writers play an important role in their motivation and confidence to learn. To feel that they have no skills to offer can be extremely discouraging when they suddenly find themselves in a new and strange environment.

One of the flaws in the particular developmental model is that it fails to acknowledge that children can be very independent in their early writing. Indeed, it could be argued that certain forms of support, for example teachers' writing for children to copy, actually presents a barrier to children's learning and slows down the impetus. Insisting that the child should copy an adult's version of what the child wants to say has three main drawbacks:

1 The child all too often perceives this as a message that their writing is not good enough; in other words, that they are not regarded by others as a real writer. This can affect confidence and limit the child's motivation to write independently.

2 The child is deprived of the opportunity to sound out and invent spellings – a process that has been proven to play a valuable part in early spelling development by helping children to consider the sounds within the parts of words.

3 The child is likely to be less experimental in the things he or she plans to write and the vocabulary he or she is likely to attempt.

Figure 8.1 The recurring principle: repeated movements, e.g. loops

Figure 8.2 The generative principle: small number of letters repeated in different combinations

Figure 8.3 The sign concept: representational drawing, awareness that print carries message, e.g. McDonald's

Figure 8.4 The flexibility principle: invention of letters, knowledge of similarities between letters leads to experimentation

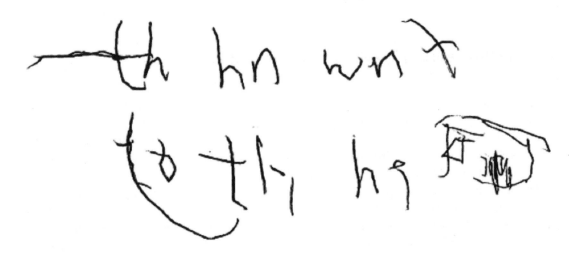

Figure 8.5 Line and page principles: directionality, left–right, top–bottom, spaces between words, words as separate units

It is therefore helpful to use a developmental framework that recognizes and empowers the child as an independent writer from the beginning and identifies the progressive features that should emerge as the child's writing develops. One example of how such a model might work is presented here.

Developmental stages of the early years independent writer

- The **emergent writer** understands the function of print and writes for different purposes in his or her play. This writing cannot normally be decoded by a reader who has not observed the process and listened to the child's accompanying talk.

- The **exploratory writer** actively relates sounds to meaning through his or her own invented spellings. This writer is confident in his or her own ideas, perceives him/herself as a writer and does not copy-write from an adult's writing above his or her own.

- The **communicative writer** writes texts that can be read by others. This writer seeks out, independently, letter and sound information from a range of sources, e.g. books, adults, other children, posters, word cards, displays. He or she will sometimes change words after they have been written.

- The **reflective writer** checks, reconsiders and redrafts his or her work. This redrafting is based on a recognition of the need for accuracy in punctuation, spelling and grammar. He or she is able to discuss his or her writing retrospectively and evaluates the effectiveness of his or her communication.

- The **versatile writer** is able to plan and adapt his or her style according to the purpose of and audience for the writing, and is able to move text around in order to reorganize his or her ideas when necessary. The majority of the writing is produced correctly, but ambitious use of extended vocabulary means that more challenging words are sometimes misspelt. Editing and redrafting will take place in order to develop the quality of the work even further.

ACTIVITY 8.1 Identifying stages of writing development   (Time: 30 minutes)

With the permission of the teacher, make a collection of photocopies of children's writing and try to match the stages of development with one or more of the models discussed so far. For the 'independent writer' model you will also need to observe the children at work to check on the processes taking place at the time of writing.

Making links between writing, reading and oracy

Texts provide models for children's writing. The discussions you have with children when they are reading, about words, spaces, letters, full stops and so on, are actively feeding into their writing (Figure 8.6). Drawing attention to features in books and other texts is an important skill of the supporting adult. Every contact with a text is an opportunity to learn about writing. Similarly, reading their writing to you shows that their writing is valued and enables you to provide support where needed.

When children are attempting their own spellings, saying and listening are crucial parts of the process. Sounding out the phonemes, having fun with rhymes and distinguishing between the beginnings and endings of words are all helping to reinforce word construction skills. It has been mentioned throughout this book that the strands of language learning are virtually inseparable. Children learn to write by speaking, listening and reading. This point is reinforced by the structure of the early learning goals for the EYFS.

Figure 8.6 Supporting children through discussing their writing

Writing in the EYFS

The EYFS provides a structured framework to support the development of children's writing (DCSF, 2008). Within the area of learning for CLL, there are three strands that relate directly to writing. You will see in Table 8.1 that the early learning goals for 'Linking sounds and letters' are just as relevant to writing as they are to reading, speaking and listening.

Table 8.1 Early learning goals related to writing development (DCSF, 2008)

Linking sounds and letters

- Hear and say sounds in words in the order in which they occur.
- Link sounds to letters, naming and sounding the letters of the alphabet.
- Use their phonic knowledge to write simple regular words and make phonetically plausible attempts at more complex words.

Writing

- Use their phonic knowledge to write simple regular words and make phonetically plausible attempts at more complex words.
- Attempt writing for different purposes, using features of different forms such as lists, stories and instructions.
- Write their own names and other things such as labels and captions, and begin to form simple sentences, sometimes using punctuation.

Handwriting

- Use a pencil and hold it effectively to form recognizable letters, most of which are correctly formed.

The inclusion of a systematic approach to the teaching of phonics is also a significant and vital element of teaching children to write. Please refer to Chapter 6 for an explanation of how this is provided in the EYFS and see the resource *Linking Letters and Sounds* (DCSF, 2007) for the detailed content of what should be taught and the sequential stages. Clearly, you need to be fully familiar with the EYFS requirements and the requirements for phonics teaching if you are working in an early years setting.

National Curriculum expectations for writing

The programme of learning for writing provides a framework for children to:

- develop essential knowledge, such as the power of language to engage the reader and express ideas;
- learn key skills such as drafting and writing to present ideas and opinions;
- use their knowledge and skills in writing across other areas of the curriculum.

The breadth of learning should enable children to:

- learn to write for a variety of purposes, for a range of audiences and in a range of forms;
- develop their understanding of how writing is essential to thinking and learning, and is enjoyable, creative and rewarding;
- explore writing using different media.

More detail of how the curriculum for writing should progress and the levels that children are expected to reach can be found on the QCDA website (www.curriculum.qcda.gov.uk).

If practitioners are to design the most appropriate activities to promote the development of knowledge and skills in writing, it is essential that they understand the different processes involved in writing.

The processes of writing

Imagine that you are looking at two stories written by seven-year-olds. One is in neatly joined handwriting, complete with full stops, capital letters and mostly correct spellings. The other is scrawled and untidy with evidence of many misspelt words. Your first impression might be that the first child is a 'better writer' than the second. Then, upon closer inspection, you note the following features:

- **Story 1** – short simple sentences, limited vocabulary, little description, muddled tenses, unclear storyline.
- **Story 2** – complex sentences with good use of conjunctions, misspelt words are nevertheless phonologically systematic and are ambitious/adventurous vocabulary, storyline is well developed with good description of characters, mood and action.

How do we begin to assess which is the better piece of writing? The answer is that we can't make a general comparison between the two. We need to separate out the different components of the writing in order to see how each child is progressing within the different skill areas. Child 1 has a well-developed style of handwriting, fluent, legible and presentable, but needs more work on sentence construction and use of vocabulary. Child 2 is a skilled storywriter and an accomplished sculptor of words, but needs to develop more control over her handwriting. This is intended to illustrate the fact that when supporting children in their writing we need to be aware of the different processes that are involved.

These two groups are sometimes called 'authorship skills' and 'secretarial skills'. Authorship skills are about style, organization, communication, development of ideas, creativity, adaptability to audience and purpose, and sensitivity to the audience. Secretarial skills include spelling, punctuation, grammar and presentation.

The art of the supporting adult is to know when it is appropriate to intervene and why. Table 8.2 illustrates how it can be appropriate to offer certain types of support at different stages of the writing process.

Table 8.2 Stages of adult support during writing processes

Adult support for secretarial	Child's writing processes	Adult support for authorship
	Planning ◄———————	—— Stimulus provision
	◄———————	—— Encouraging discussion
	First draft ◄———————	Encourage independence
Suggest focus for checks ——► Checking back ◄——————— (e.g. full stops)		—— Respond to meaning
	◄———————	—— Ask questions
	◄———————	—— Read together
Child checks spellings ——► Redrafting ◄——————— with support		Encourage independence
Reads aloud for accuracy ——► Correcting		
Evaluates presentation ——►		
Revise handwriting rules ——► Final draft ◄———————		Reminder of purpose
Reminder of reader's needs ——►		

Supporting children's spelling

Adults, particularly parents, can sometimes have very unreasonable expectations of children's spellings. One way of tuning in to the ability level children are at with their spelling is to relate it to a developmental framework for spelling.

Gentry (1994) proposes that children's spelling moves through five identifiable stages:

1 **Precommunicative stage** where the child writes down random shapes, letters and numbers to represent meaning. This is unlikely to be legible to another reader.

2 **Semiphonetic stage** where the child represents whole chunks of sounds with single letters, e.g. fm=farm, tct=tractor.

3 **Phonetic stage** where the child introduces vowels and represents most of the sounds phonetically, e.g. camru=camera, sestu=sister.

4 **Transitional stage** where the child starts to demonstrate a knowledge of spelling patterns and rules, e.g. trolly=trolley, powny=pony.

5 **Correct stage** where the child has a good understanding of spelling rules, can apply these to attempts at new words, and visualize and say spellings before writing them down.

This model is particularly helpful when assessing children's writing because it provides a clear diagnostic framework for teachers in Key Stage 1 when they are planning a spelling programme. It also helps adults to decipher what children are writing and understand the level of their approach.

Spelling involves a complex set of brain processes. These include what we see, what we hear, what we remember and how we feel the directional movement of our pen. It is therefore appropriate that spelling is taught with these multisensory skills in mind, and teachers usually employ a range of methods to help children to develop their spelling vocabulary.

Adults who are assisting children in their writing need to consider the following when providing additional support for spelling:

- Respect children's own attempts.
- Clap the rhythms of the words to identify the syllables.
- Play and have fun with words and sounds.

- Note any patterns in their mistakes and prioritize what they need to learn next.
- Always encourage the children to have a go first before writing a word for them.
- Help the children to say the sounds aloud and think about the order of those sounds.
- Draw on the children's existing alphabet knowledge.
- Draw attention to the parts of words (chunks).
- Encourage the use of memory (look and cover).
- Practise the 'feel' of letter groups (linking with handwriting).
- Link writing to reading.
- Write three versions of a word for children to choose the correct version.
- Make links with other similar words.
- Discourage dictionaries at the first-draft stage.
- Encourage dictionaries at the redraft stage.
- Let the children highlight words that need correcting – they usually do know.
- Explain that spotting mistakes isn't a sign of failure, it is a sign of success.
- Let the children see you using a dictionary sometimes – we all need them!

Handwriting

Handwriting should be taught correctly from an early stage and schools will have a clearly defined handwriting policy. Habits, once formed, are very hard to change, so getting it right from the start is important. Supporting adults should ensure that they are familiar with the nursery or school policy so that they are modelling the correct approach to letter formation and strokes. Handwriting is a motor skill that has to be taught and practised. It is such a physical part of the writing process that individual checking and support is usually needed. The following checklist is designed to help you with this task:

- Is the child sitting comfortably?
- Can the child see his or her paper?
- How is the child holding his or her pencil?
- Is the child leaving spaces between words?
- Is the child recognizing the heights of tall and upper-case letters?
- Are the letter formations in line with the school policy?

In addition, if the child is left-handed:

- Does the child have enough elbow room?
- Are they sitting to the left of their neighbour?
- Is the paper to the child's left, tilted slightly so he or she can see the writing?
- Are you demonstrating in a way that is possible with the left hand?
- Are you allowing the child enough time?

ACTIVITY 8.2 How does it feel to learn to write?　　　　　　　　**(Time: 5 minutes)**

Using Activity Sheet N, make a copy of the text using the hand that you don't normally use for writing. Discuss with others how that feels.

Writing and play

Writing activities can have a very appropriate place within children's play activities, particularly if they are a natural progression of the play initiated by the child (Figure 8.7). When playing, a child is usually in charge of the decision-making and therefore the writing is driven by the child's motivation or need to write. However, the likelihood of the child making that choice is also dependent upon the quality of planning by practitioners. If there is a message pad and pen by the telephone in the home corner, he or she is far more likely to write a 'message' than if there is not. Many settings have a writing area, where children can use the resources to write for any purpose they have identified – this might spring from other areas of play (e.g. making a bill for the car the child has just repaired), or might be a discrete writing activity (e.g. writing a letter to Goldilocks). Such writing areas work well where there is a variety of resources such as:

- different shapes of paper;
- different coloured paper;
- different sizes of paper;
- scrap paper and best paper;
- lined paper and plain paper;
- envelopes;
- book-making resources;
- folders;
- range of writing implements (including pens);
- pencil sharpeners;
- rubbers;
- stencils;
- hole punchers;
- labels;
- typewriters;
- post box;
- words on display;
- examples of texts;
- dictionaries and thesauruses.

Figure 8.7 Play provides valuable contexts for writing

Children should have free access to these resources but should also be taught how to use them correctly and leave the area tidy. Modelling the writing process by taking part in the role play can help you to structure children's play into more purposeful learning activities. The questions you ask and references you make to other things will all help to support and extend children's writing.

ACTIVITY 8.3 Writing in role   **(Time: 15 minutes)**

Make a list of the types of writing opportunities that could be provided in four different role play corners. Consider the types of intervention you could make to extend the children's skills and knowledge of writing.

Writing on the computer

Writing on a computer offers children excellent opportunities to link reading and writing (Figure 8.8). It also encourages children to edit easily, and produce a presentable piece of text. All children should be taught computer skills from an early age if they are to be prepared for the technological society in which we live. When supporting children at the computer try to encourage them to:

- use all their fingers for typing;
- use their thumbs for the space bar;
- write first then edit;
- print out and highlight corrections;
- read back their own work to you or to another child;
- store their work and come back to it later where appropriate.

Figure 8.8 Computers provide valuable reading and writing opportunities for young children

Writing across the areas of learning

There are reasons for children to write in many areas of the curriculum (Table 8.3). Variety offers children the opportunity to write in different ways and for different purposes. And it can simply be fun, especially when experimenting with different media. Children are much more motivated to write when:

- it is part of an interesting or fun activity;
- they have a good reason for writing;
- there is an interested audience waiting for their writing;
- they have something to write about;
- the writing is likely to elicit a response or reply;
- they have resources to stimulate their writing;
- they feel safe to experiment.

Table 8.3 Types of writing across the curriculum

Activity	Area of learning	Format
Collect and draw mini-beasts	KUW	Chart
Word games	CLL	Lists
Seasons word play	KUW	Word collages List poems Shape poems
Clothes lists	PSED	List
Weather recording	KUW	Diary
Book-making	Various	Books
Sequencing and writing	Various	Story
Cooking	KUW	Recipe card
Model-making	CD	Plan or list
Diagrams	Various	Labels
Messages to...	Various	Letters
Puppet plays	CLL	Story scripts
Greetings cards	PSED	Card
Write to people in hospital	PSED	Letter
Instructions for a game	Various	Ordered list
Word trees	Various	One word per leaf
Recycling sorting	KUW	Chart
Advertising/appeals	KUW	Posters
Paper-making	CD	Reporting
Class newspaper	CLL	Ads, news, class
Joke book	CLL	Page layout
Role play	Various	Various
Sorting	MD	Recording
Shape	MD	Description

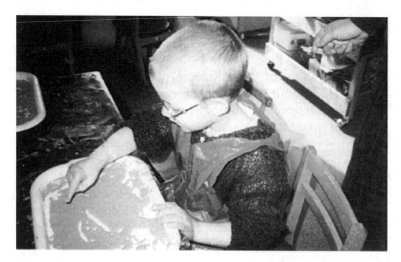

Figure 8.9 Writing can take place in a variety of media and it is fun to experiment!

Many of these activities will be familiar to you and you will no doubt know many more. The National Curriculum stresses the importance of this sort of *range* in children's writing. They should have opportunities to write in different ways for different reasons and for a variety of audiences. This includes writing in different formats and also in different styles. Confidence, fluency and accuracy are listed as key skills, and pupils should also be given opportunities to plan and review their writing. Punctuation, spelling and handwriting are each outlined in particular, as are Standard English and knowledge about language.

ACTIVITY 8.4 Writing for a purpose   **(Time: 20 minutes)**

On a piece of paper, make a list of the different purposes, audiences and forms for writing which you have observed in the settings where you work. Which do you notice the children enjoying the most? Why do you think that is the case?

Collaborative writing

Collaborative writing is not just about writing in groups or pairs; it is also about the nature of the writing process. When writing in isolation, ideas are restricted to your independent thinking – sometimes this is necessary. But when discussing ideas with others, additional thoughts can be triggered, giving the child more to write about.

The collaborative writer might consult:

- pupils
- teachers
- parents
- other adults
- editors
- books

in order to obtain:

- feedback
- advice
- information
- ideas
- comment
- other resources
- previous work
- dictionaries
- thesauruses
- other texts.

Collaboration enhances the learning benefits of the overall process. Supporting adults can be there for consultation, but should also be aware of these other places where the children should be encouraged to seek out what they need. Actively encouraging children to make their own decisions about such collaboration makes an important contribution to children's developing thinking, confidence and independence.

Responding to children's writing

The ways in which you respond to children's writing will undoubtedly have an impact on what they attempt next. For older children, settings will have different approaches to the ways in which children's work is 'corrected', but for those who play a supporting role, the following guidelines provide a framework for response that is designed to encourage and extend learning in order to improve children's writing:

- Respond to the content first.
- Show an interest in the writing.
- Ask the child about the subject matter.
- Ask the child what he or she thinks of the writing.
- Read the writing together.
- Praise the attempts at spellings before pointing out they are wrong.
- Do not overload the child with too many mistakes to think about (i.e. consider what is most appropriate for the child to learn next).
- Ask if the child would like to change or check anything.
- Ask the child what they think they could do even better next time.

Where possible, it is useful to write a response to the child. This enables the writing and reading to interlink in a very meaningful way but also enables you to model the spellings the child has not yet learned. Figure 8.10 demonstrates how the adult has responded to the child's writing by showing interest, asking a question and also modelling some of the words the child misspelt.

Giving children encouragement is not just designed to keep them happy; it is a way of ensuring that they will want to try again rather than feeling they have failed or are not capable of the task in hand. Encouragement can be given for:

- having a go;
- using interesting words;
- changing and correcting own writing;
- checking a word;

Figure 8.10 Responding and modelling

- experimenting with new ideas;
- taking the initiative;
- evaluating and improving their own writing.

ACTIVITY 8.5 Evaluating your own practice

Use Activity Sheet O to evaluate aspects of your own practice. Do not overload yourself with too many questions at once. Wherever possible, discuss these with the teacher, manager or trainer, and where necessary, list some action points on the back of the sheet. Plan to revisit these at a later date to monitor your progress.

Notes for group leaders

Extending the listed activities

- Activity 8.1 – Ask the students to bring in the samples collected and compare them. Discuss the features and stages of development and what certain children might need to learn next in terms of their writing.
- Activity 8.2 – Discuss to see how it felt. What are the implications for where the paper is positioned when two children are writing together?
- Activity 8.3 – In pairs, plan and make writing resources for a role play corner.
- Activity 8.4 – Discuss in the larger group.

Activities for assessment

- Activity 8.1 provides scope for an extended study into further developmental models. Use of the children's examples could be part of the exemplification.

- Activity 8.3 could be extended into the actual design and provision of a role play area in a setting. A written account of this could be assessed with photographic evidence, plus observations of the subsequent learning that took place through observations.

Additional topics for group discussions

- Discuss examples of stages of learning that you have observed as listed in 'Development Matters' for the writing strands of CLL.
- Share examples of handwriting and spelling policies that you have seen in different settings.
- Talk about your own experiences of learning to write.
- Why is it important for teachers to assess writing against national standards at the end of Key Stage 1?

Further reading

Bennet, J. and Hailstone, P. (2007) *The Handwriting Pocketbook.* Alresford: Teachers' Pocketbooks.

Clay, M. M. (1975) *What Did I Write?* Auckland: Heinemann Educational Books.

DCSF (2007) *Linking Letters and Sounds: Principles and Practice of High Quality Phonics.* London: DCSF Publications.

DCSF (2008) *The Early Years Foundation Stage* (Pack and CD-ROM). Nottingham: DCSF Publications.

Gentry, J. R. (1994) *Spel...is a Four-letter Word.* Oxford: Heinemann Educational Publishers.

Hall, N. and Robinson, A. (2003) *Exploring Writing and Play in the Early Years.* London: David Fulton Publishers.

Morrow, L. (2008) *Literacy Development in the Early Years: Helping Children Read and Write.* Harlow: Pearson Publishing.

Sassoon, R. (2003) *Handwriting: The Way to Teach It.* London: Sage.

Zutell, J. (2002) *Teaching and Assessing Spelling: Theory and Practice.* Leamington Spa: Scholastic.

Activity sheets

The sheets on the following pages may be photocopied for use in activities and study. This includes the reproduction of more than one copy by purchasing institutions for educational purposes within that institution only.

Language communities

Choose three of the language communities from the list in Figure 1.2 in Chapter 1. In the three sections below list the differences between them by thinking about particular vocabulary and the different purposes of the language. The first example has been completed for you.

SITUATION: shops

Vocabulary	Purposes
basket	asking about or comparing products
trolley	describing different foods
bag	reading adverts and labels
shopping list	planning future meals
shelves	describing likes and dislikes
packets	explaining
bigger, heavier	decision-making

SITUATION:

Vocabulary	Purposes

SITUATION:

Vocabulary	Purposes

SITUATION:

Vocabulary	Purposes

Play and language

Try to observe different children in the same situation OR the same child in different situations. Use a copy of this sheet for each observation.

Play activity	
Types of language the child is using	
How is the language helping the thinking?	
Is the child looking at or writing texts? This might include labels, computer and other such resources – not necessarily books	

ACTIVITY SHEET C
Different types of partnerships

Think about partnerships that you have observed in a setting where you have worked OR think about potential partnerships. What impact have they had, or could they have, on outcomes for children? For example, how well they:

- achieve;
- enjoy learning;
- behave;
- stay and feel safe;
- are healthy and (where appropriate) make healthy choices;
- develop skills for their future economic well-being;
- contribute to their school/setting and local community.

Record your thoughts on the sheet. An example has been completed for you and some parts of columns have also been completed.

Type of partnership	Example	Action	Actual or potential impact
Team within setting			
			Improved behaviour
Parent/carer			
Local authority agency	Speech therapist	Sharing of strategies	Improved language skills
Other local services	Fire service		
With local businesses		Guided visit to local supermarket	

ACTIVITY SHEET D
Evaluating your working partnerships

Think about your main current working partnership. If you are not currently employed, try to recall a partnership from a previous post, or with a fellow trainee.

What qualities do you think you bring to this partnership?

What qualities does the other person bring to the partnership?

What is the worst problem you have encountered in this partnership?

How did you deal with this?

In retrospect, how might you have responded differently, if that was possible?

How do you usually respond to criticism from other people?

Think of an area of your work that you think could be improved. Make a negative statement about it here as if it were being said in a highly critical way.

Try to think of a positive response to the criticism, perhaps identifying three action points to follow.

Now try to find someone with whom you can discuss your responses to this activity. Decide first what you want to gain from the discussion.

Child observations

Child's name: _____

In a pair

Date: _____   Context: _____

In a small group (e.g. 3 or 4)

Date: _____   Context: _____

Whole-class situation (e.g. storytime)

Date: _____   Context: _____

One-to-one with an adult

Date: _____   Context: _____

Getting to know another language

Choose another language that is common in the area where you work or live. Find out as much as you can about the language and culture. Try to talk to a parent about their expectations for their child and how the setting can help.

Language and culture	
Common greetings	
Other useful phrases	
Popular foods	
Religion	
Other traditions (e.g. dress, music)	
What do parents say about how they want their child to learn?	

ACTIVITY SHEET G
Bilingual group observations

With the permission of the person in charge, conduct a range of five-minute observations of bilingual children working in groups of different sizes, including pairs. The schedule below is designed to make your recording easier, but you may wish to design a different format. Try to observe from a distance, otherwise you will be drawn into the activity!

As you observe, note down the type of talk for each child as it happens using the following codes: E= explaining, Q=questioning, A=answering, R=repeating, D=describing. At the end your entries might look like this:

CHILD A: E E E Q A A A A A A

If they used their home language, place a circle round the letter.

ACTIVITY AREA:

RESOURCES:

HOME LANGUAGE: CHILD A   CHILD B

CHILD C   CHILD D

CHILD E   CHILD F

CHILD A:

CHILD B:

CHILD C:

CHILD D:

CHILD E:

CHILD F:

When your observations are complete, look at them carefully and note any patterns or differences between the different situations. Make a list of four points you feel might influence your future practice as a result of conducting this exercise.

Analysing your own talk

Think back to a certain time yesterday and imagine that your day was recorded on DVD from that point! In the first two columns below, record as much of the talk as you can remember by mentally recalling the order of events and the people to whom you spoke. It might help to do this chronologically.

Next, try to examine each example more closely by listing the *reason* for your talk and what sort of talk it was. Two examples have been given to guide you.

Situation	Person	Example	Type of talk
On the bus	Driver	Asking for a ticket	Request
Arriving at work	Friend at work	News about last night	Recalling/retelling

Encouraging different types of talk

On page 40 of Chapter 5, you have been reading about the different types of talk that children might use to extend their range. However, their ability to do this can depend very much on the quality of opportunities that you provide. Taking each of the examples below, plan an activity that will use that specific type of talk. Think about what resources will help the children and what input you will make to promote each type of talk.

Explaining

Describe the activity:

Resources to encourage the talk:

How will your own talk help the children to EXPLAIN?

Giving instructions

Describe the activity:

Resources to encourage the talk:

How will your own talk help the children to GIVE INSTRUCTIONS?

Describing

Describe the activity:

Resources to encourage the talk:

How will your own talk help the children to DESCRIBE?

What do I do when I read?

On the chart below, make notes about how you read the different types of text listed.

Text	What do I do when I read this?
Celebrity gossip magazine	
Yellow Pages	
Results from a search engine	
Recipe	
Newspaper	
Junk mail	
Party political leaflets	
Personal letter	
News item with difficult and unusual foreign names	
Home page of a social networking site	
TV guide	
Special offers	
Text on your mobile phone	

Analysing your own reading strategies

Below you will find four unusual examples of text. Cover these up immediately without looking at them. One at a time, uncover the texts and try to read them. Make notes after each one of the strategies you have used to decipher and understand what is written.

Text 1

The fat cat was too large to squeeze through the cat flap.

Text 2

Lxst wxxk I vxsxtxed my mxthxr xnd fxthxr. I dxdnt knxw thxt my sxstxr wxs xlsx gxxng tx bx thxrx. Wx hxd x gxxd chxt bxcxxsx wx hxdnt sxxn xxch xthxr fxr x lxng txmx.

Text 3

viss iss u spilink lisst ken u reid ve wudz buk knighs trea soopa pownd phinnish throo seeling benniffitt skweez schoopeed owver reesint bredd

Text 4

Little Rid Redong Hud was unsure about which path she should take. The volvo was chasing her down one path and the mad woodkiller down the other. If only she could reach her granddaughter's house. Then she would be quiet safe. The sound of the volvo's engine revving became louder and louder. The woodpecker's cries were blood-curdling. There was only one thing left to do. She must find the mobile home and phone her mother.

Getting to know a reader

Please consult with the teacher or manager before doing this task. It is important that you choose the child together and that no unusual pressure or demands are placed upon the child. The activity is intended to strengthen your understanding of what is happening when children read so that you can provide appropriate support.

Child: _____   **Date:** _____

Book: _____

Child's attitudes to reading

Child's attitudes to books

What does the child know already about books?

    Author
    Title
    Pages
    Front/back
    Left to right
    Top to bottom
    What is a word?
    What is a letter?
    Spaces
    Full stops

Words that caused problems on this occasion

Letters that caused a problem on this occasion

Strategies used to tackle unknown words

Use of contextual clues

Ability to recall the story sequentially

Discussion of own experiences relating to story

Reading opportunities across areas of learning

Consider the following situations in a nursery and jot down ideas for resources and types of adult intervention to support and develop aspects of children's reading.

Situation	Resources	Intervention
Sand play		
Water area		
Role play office area		
Writing corner		
Model-making		
Visit from the police		
Cooking		
Growing vegetables		
Local walk		
Using plasticine		
Computer		

© Suzi Clipson-Boyles, *Supporting Language and Literacy 0–5*, 3rd edn. London: Routledge, 2010.

How does it feel to learn to write?

This task is designed to help you understand how a child feels when he or she is learning to write. Using the hand which you do not normally use for writing, make a copy of the text on the top half of the page by writing on the bottom half of the page. Make a note of how it feels and of any changes you needed to make in order to compensate.

Why did Mr Fish (an acquaintance of George Bernard Shaw) like to spell his name in a more interesting way?

Mr GHOTIUGH

GH = f as in tough
O = i as in women
TI = sh as in initial
UGH = silent as in though

YOUR COPY...

ACTIVITY SHEET O

Reflecting on your own practices

During the course of one week, try to focus on two questions from the list below. Use the process to identify any areas in which you might like to seek further advice from the teacher. Make a list of action points on the back of a photocopy of this sheet.

- When a child asks you for a spelling, what things can you do to encourage independence and confidence?

- When do you ask children to read their writing to you?

- How do you respond to the content of children's writing?

- How do you focus on the good elements before pointing out the mistakes?

- How do you point out mistakes and when is it necessary to limit the number of mistakes to be discussed with the child?

- How might you encourage the child to discuss other ideas of his or her own?

- How do you suggest new ideas to the child without taking over the ownership of the work?

- How do you show children that you value their contributions?

- If a child offers a totally wrong answer how do you respond so that he or she does not feel embarrassed or discouraged?

- How can you set mini-targets to help a child through a much larger task?

- When children are practising handwriting, do you observe the strokes?

Index